THE STORY OF SALE FROM 1806 TO 1876

A "House Detective" Book

by

John Newhill

First published in 2000
By John Newhill, 25 Amberley Road, Sale, Cheshire M33 6QP

© John Newhill 2000
ISBN 0 9537862 0 X

Typeset by Northern Writers Advisory Services, Sale, Cheshire

Printed by Intype (London) Ltd

All rights reserved.

All photographs and maps are by the author, except the photograph on the front cover. This view of School Road, taken towards the end of the nineteenth century, was reprinted with the kind permission of the Trafford Local Studies Centre.

CONTENTS

Introduction		5
1.	Sale and Ashton in 1806	9
2.	Land and property ownership	19
3.	Population and occupations	23
4.	(i) Events in Sale, 1806-76 (ii) National events, 1806-76 (iii) The railway (1849)	26
5.	The Development of Central Sale, 1806-76 (between Broad Road and Marsland Road) The Area in 1806; 1806-1841; 1841-1861; 1861-1876	31
6.	The Development of Northern Sale, 1806-76 (north of Chapel Road and Broad Road) The Area in 1806; 1806-1841; 1841-1861; 1861-1876	72
7.	The Development of Southern Sale, 1806-76 (Marsland Road and the area south) The Area in 1806; 1806-1841; 1841-1861; 1861-1876	93
8.	The Development of Eastern Sale, 1806-76 (east of the 'Legh Arms' and Old Hall Road) The Area in 1806; 1806-1841; 1841-1861; 1861-1876	115
Appendices	(i) Farms in Sale (ii) Large houses (iii) Origins of street names	134 145 149

Bibliography	150
General Index	152
Surname Index	156
House Name Index	162

ILLUSTRATIONS

Photographs

1.	Poor Rate Notice, July 1860	13
2.	'Lime Place', Northenden Road	38
3.	'Warburton House', Britannia Grove	48
4.	'Aroma Terrace', Wardle Road	50
5.	'Strawberry Bank', Northenden Road	60
6.	'Yew Tree Cottage', Broad Road	76
7.	'Ivy Cottage', Clarendon Crescent	79
8.	Houses on Marsland Road	94
9.	'Woodheys', Washway Road	98
10.	'Raglan House', Raglan Road	100
11.	'Brookside', Washway Road	106
12.	'Belmore', Brooklands Road	110
13.	'Brooklands Cottage', Marsland Road	112
14.	'Yew Tree Cottage', Northenden Road	119

Maps

1.	Sale, Ashton and the surrounding area in the early nineteenth century	8
2.	Sale in 1806	10
3.	Parish boundaries in Ashton and Sale in the first half of the nineteenth century	
4.	Land ownership in Sale in 1806	18
5.	Sale divided into four areas for the purpose of this book	30
6.	Sale centre in 1860	33
7.	Farms south of Moor Nook & Northenden Road in 1806	92
8.	Farms in eastern Sale in 1806	116

INTRODUCTION

Sitting down to write a history of Sale, one is faced with a major difficulty - nothing of significance happened. No battles or nationally-important events ever took place in Ashton or Sale. Two thousand years of their history may be summed up in the following thirty-two words: 'The Romans built a road, the Saxons built two settlements, the road was later turnpiked, a canal and railway were near to it and a once agricultural village became a residential suburb'. A history of Ashton and Sale must therefore concentrate on buildings and personalities. I believe that the story of the development from fields to suburban housing is worth telling for four reasons - (i) I am sure that many of the present-day inhabitants of Sale would like to know more about the history of their town, and are curious to know when their road was built, how it got its name, and who lived there in the past, (ii) the names of the people who created Sale in the nineteenth century should be known to their descendants, (iii) the overall story will be of interest to local historians in general, and (iv) it seems right and proper that, having spent years amassing a great deal of information about Sale's past from old documents, I should make this available to future researchers.

In my book *Sale, Cheshire, in 1841* (published in 1994) I gave a detailed picture of Sale and Ashton-on-Mersey in 1841, based on the 1841 census and the three Tithe Apportionments of approximately the same date. I then began to research the development of the two townships in the Victorian era, intending to produce a book describing the growth of Sale and Ashton in the period 1841 to 1880. The re-discovery of the Pre-Enclosure Map of Sale in Trafford Local Studies Centre made me realise that I could now go back thirty-five years before 1841 and cover the seventy years from 1806 to the date of the first large-scale Ordnance Survey map (1876). There were two large-scale maps of Sale drawn up at the time of the Enclosure of Sale Moor in 1806-7. The Pre-Enclosure Map, drawn by Edward Mason of Chorlton, shows the township of Sale in 1806 at a scale of 20.91 inches to the mile. Very similar to the later Tithe Apportionment maps, it shows each field and building, and at the bottom of the map there is a schedule giving the names of all owners and occupiers with the area of their holdings. Even the separate gates into the various fields are shown. Because of its age, however, many of the field and house numbers (in red ink on the map) have faded and are decipherable only with a great amount of trouble and care. The Post-Enclosure Map is again by Edward Mason, and is basically the 1806 map repeated, with Sale Moor (the area to be enclosed) now divided up into parcels of land. The Post-Enclosure Schedule is a separate booklet, and the areas given are in acres, rods and poles, whereas the schedule on the Pre-Enclosure Map lists field areas in acres and decimals of an acre. The whereabouts of the original of the Post-Enclosure Map are not known, but both Manchester Central Library and Trafford Local Studies Centre have quarter-size photocopies. By spending many hours using a magnifying glass on both maps (Pre- and Post-Enclosure), however, I have been able identify all the houses and over 95% of the fields.

I was lucky in also having a later map to work with. This was the map of Sale in 1860 prepared by William Wilson at the request of the Township Vestry. The scale is 26.5 inches to the mile. Unfortunately the accompanying reference book has not survived.

In this book I intend to describe the development of Sale from 1806 to 1876. I shall try to create a picture of the township and its inhabitants between these two dates. Readers will understand that because of the restraints of space this account cannot be as detailed as the description given in *Sale, Cheshire, in 1841*, where every house and most families were mentioned. For this reason, although the building of each house between 1806 and 1876 will be covered, it is impracticable to discuss every inhabitant. Many of the people described will be craftsmen, professionals or property-owners, as there is more information available about their lives and activities, and they also tended to be less mobile.

The information given in *Sale, Cheshire, in 1841* obviously fits into the middle of this book. After some consideration I have decided merely to refer to it where necessary. To readers who do not have a copy, I apologise in advance for any frustration caused, but they must agree that it would be impractical to repeat all the information.

First I intend to set the scene by describing Sale in 1806; then I shall list events which were relevant to the township during the 70 years from 1806 to 1876. Events which were peculiar to a certain area will be dealt with in the following chapters. As a background I shall also list the main national events over the same period. I have divided Sale into four areas (see map, p.30). Each of these areas is described separately.

Originally I intended to deal with Ashton-upon-Mersey also, but this has proved impracticable for two reasons - (i) the necessary documents (the rate books) have been lost and (ii) I estimate that, even using the small amount of available information to produce a much less detailed account, publication would be delayed by at least eighteen months.

It is interesting to note that in the 35 years between 1806 and 1841 there was very little change; life went on more or less as it had done for over a hundred years. The 35 years after 1841 on the other hand show great changes in the township, primarily the result of the coming of the railway in 1849.

Readers may note that there are fewer details in this book about personalities living before 1841. This is because the censuses of 1801 to 1831, which would give us these details, were destroyed. Other gaps in the records are (i) between 1831 (the last Land Tax Return) and 1836 (the first extant Poor Rate Book) and (ii) the years 1852-5 in the Rate Books.

Sharp-eyed readers who have read *Sale, Cheshire, in 1841* may notice that a few facts stated in this book differ from those given in that publication. These are cases where further research has yielded new information.

I would like to disabuse the reader of the idea that collecting the information for this book has been merely a matter of copying out entries from old documents. The Land Tax lists contain no addresses at all; the early censuses and directories contain very few, and these are vague. Likewise, the rate books give only general addresses - for example, 'Moor Lane' refers to this road and all the small roads leading off. This means that it often happened that I knew that a new house was built on a certain road, but had no indication of which house it was. The house numbering system was not introduced in Sale until 1871, and even then over the next ten years the numbers were rarely used. In several cases it has been necessary to trace all the houses on a certain road backwards from 1888 (the first street directory) through thirty or forty years to find exactly which ones were the first to be built.

In the Rate Books properties were listed in alphabetical order of *occupiers' names* until 1858. After this they were listed in alphabetical order of *owners' names*. This means that if either the owner or the occupier changed, it was necessary to look through anywhere up to 1500 names to find the new owner or occupant. Tracing the locations of various houses, and finding who lived there and when has at some times seemed like a problem worthy of the mental processes of a Hercule Poirot.

I have given dates of birth and death of people mentioned, wherever it has been possible to ascertain them. Dates accompanied by an asterisk are estimated from ages given in census returns, or from ages quoted on grave-stones.

The decision to be comprehensive, in other words to include every house in my narrative, has two disadvantages. Firstly, it was no longer possible to pick out the more interesting stories and neglect the mundane; secondly, it meant that awkward problems could not be quietly omitted - they had to be solved, however long this took.

I would like to offer my thanks to the staff of Trafford Local History Centre for their help and patience. Sometimes I have asked for the same Rate Books on three or four occasions as I tried to re-check my facts. I must also thank my wife, Jean, for her forbearance as I disappeared yet again to the Library. I must admit that the point was reached where she said, 'Surely you've read every book in that library by now.' Lastly, I must thank members of the Ashton and Sale History Society for information given, especially Peter Hughes, who told me where to find information on the Bellhouse family, Alan Morrison, whose gift of copies of maps set me going in the first place, and George Cogswell, who generously let me see the information he had gathered on the Moor Nook area.

John Newhill, Sale 1999

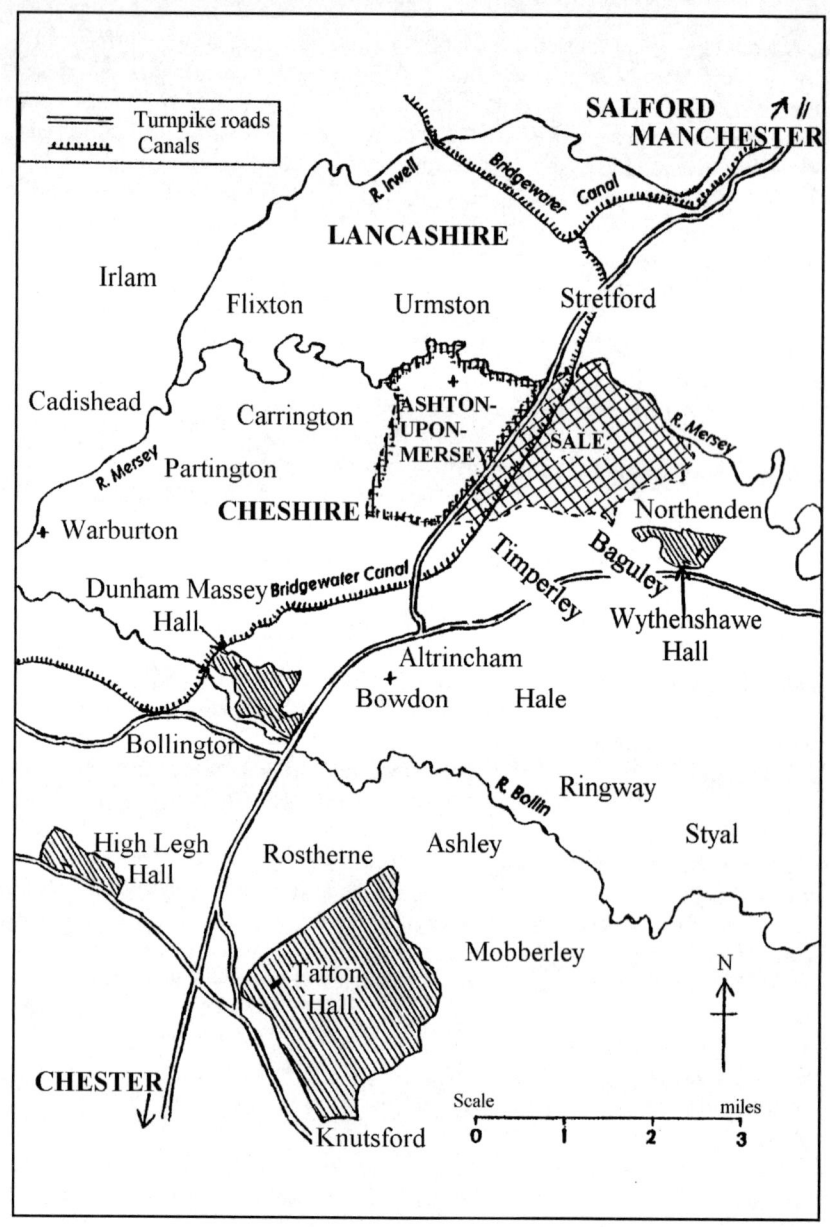

Sale, Ashton and the surrounding area in the early nineteenth century.

1. ASHTON and SALE IN 1806

Britain in 1806

Older readers who remember the Second World War will have some appreciation of the position in which Britain found herself at the beginning of 1806. The independent nations of Europe were being conquered one by one by a dictator; in 1806 he was French - Napoleon Bonaparte. Britain and France had been at war for nine years, apart from a short truce in 1802-3. The threat of invasion from France had led to the formation of local militias, a prime example being the Ashton-upon-Mersey and Sale Volunteer Force, which was formed by John Moore junior in 1803 with himself as Captain. Volunteers signed on at the Plough Inn in Ashton. In answer to the French threat, the British Navy tried to prevent neutral ships trading with France, and also inflicted a number of defeats on the French Fleet, the latest being in November 1805, at Trafalgar. The British Prime Minister, William Pitt the Younger, died in January 1806 and this led to a number of squabbles among the ruling Tory party. Although King George III had been on the throne for over 45 years, it was only 60 years since Bonnie Prince Charlie had thrown England and Scotland into turmoil by his attempt to regain the throne for his father James Stewart. George, the Prince of Wales, was involved in an extremely acrimonious divorce battle with his wife, Caroline.

Topography

The two urban districts of Ashton-on-Mersey and Sale were joined together in October 1930, making one urban district roughly 3½ miles from west to east and 2 miles from north to south. Situated on the North Cheshire Plain five miles south-west of the centre of Manchester, Ashton-on-Mersey and Sale had been separated for hundreds of years by the old Roman Road from Chester to Manchester. The road formed the boundary between the townships, the centres of which lay approximately three-quarters of a mile to the west and east of the road. Both townships were Saxon settlements - 'Ashton' being 'the farm or hamlet near the ash trees' and 'Sale' meaning 'at the willows'.

The northern boundary of both townships was the River Mersey, which flows westwards at this point, forming the boundary in Saxon times between Mercia and Northumberland, and later between Cheshire and Lancashire. (Some minor deviations between the river and the county boundary are discussed in *Sale, Cheshire in 1841*, pages 1 and 2.) The southern boundary of both townships was a small brook which had a different name in each of the townships it traversed on its way to join the Mersey. In Sale it was 'Baguley Brook', and in Ashton it became 'Sinderland Brook'; further west in Carrington and Partington, where it ran into the Mersey, it was 'Red Brook'. There were a number of other small streams in the area. Barrow Brook ran through

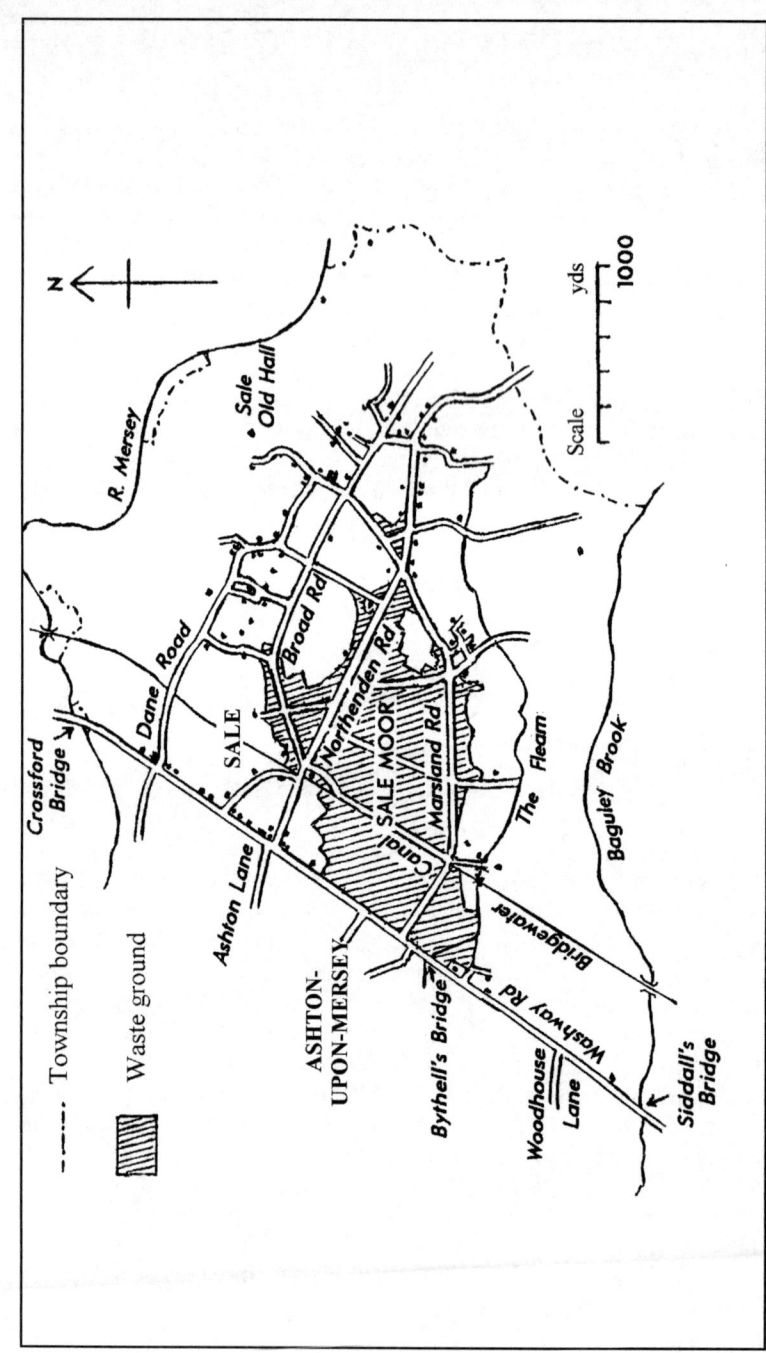

Sale in 1806

the flood-plain between Dane Road and the Mersey, joining the latter just inside the Ashton boundary. Button Brook (or 'The Fleam') ran westwards from near Wythenshawe Hall through Sale and Ashton to join the Mersey in Carrington, just beyond the Ashton boundary (see the article in the *Ashton and Sale History Society Newsletter*, number 3, November 1993). This is now completely culverted and few people are aware of its existence. One other smaller stream ('Stromford Brook') ran westwards between Glebelands Road and the Mersey. As the main road runs from south-west to north-east three bridges were necessary to cross the larger streams (Barrow Brook seems to have been culverted under the A56 at an early date). Two of the bridges, 'Crossford Bridge' over the Mersey and 'Siddall's Bridge' over Baguley Brook, are well-known to local inhabitants, but the third bridge, 'Bythell's Bridge' (150 yards south of the junction of Marsland Road and Washway Road) is completely unknown today, as there is now no indication that a stream flows under the road at this point.

The eastern boundary of Sale was another small stream which could possibly have been the original course of Baguley Brook. Over the years this stream had become silted up and a hedge ('Sale Hedge') had grown along it during the last half of the eighteenth century. The western boundary of Ashton ran along the edge of Carrington Moss. Its position was the subject of a certain amount of dispute, and an artificially straight line appears to have been fixed in the 1840's.

The whole area is extremely flat. The western extremity of Ashton is 70 feet above sea-level; Washway Road (the boundary between Ashton and Sale) lies 79 feet above sea-level, and the ground rises only 18 feet in the 2½ miles to the eastern boundary of Sale. Gaps between buildings occasionally yield glimpses of the Pennines, low grey hills some fifteen miles to the east and north.

In general the soil is a good, sandy loam, which has been the basis of the many farms and market gardens in the area.

Sale Moor

There is some evidence that the whole of Sale and Ashton-upon-Mersey were originally covered by Carrington Moss, which stretched as far as Wythenshawe Hall. Over the centuries land had been slowly enclosed and turned into farmland. In 1806 the waste land at the centre of Sale ('Sale Moor') still covered 280 acres (15% of the township's total area). Roughly triangular in shape, it almost filled the whole area between School Road and Raglan Road in the west, and Baguley Road in the east. The area was 800 yards from north to south and 2000 yards from west to east. Several open tracks or paths through the Moor had existed for a number of years; these are shown as dotted lines on the Legh Estate Map of 1801, and when the Moor was enclosed in 1806-7 they were made into proper roads (the Enclosure Award of 1807 describes them as 'now staked out and formed'). These new roads were straight and included Northenden Road, Irlam Road, Hope Road, Wardle Road and Derbyshire

Road (they had different names in 1806). When the Moor was enclosed, the poorer people suffered, as they lost land upon which they had been able to graze a few cattle or pigs. Many could no longer sustain an independent existence, and were compelled to become labourers working for someone else. Landowners on the other hand gained, as each one was alloted a portion of the newly-enclosed land, roughly in proportion to his or her existing holding.

Transport

There were two means of transport available in 1806. These were the canal and the roads.

The Bridgewater Canal

The Duke of Bridgewater's Canal was originally built to convey coal from the mines near Worsley to the town of Manchester. The 26-mile extension from Stretford through Sale and Altrincham to Runcorn was started in 1763. For many years 1765 was taken as the opening date of the canal through Sale and Altrincham, and this date has been quoted by earlier authors (e.g. Swain and Massey). Modern research, however, indicates that the canal was not opened from Cornbrook to Altrincham until June 1766. It was another ten years before the canal was finally completed through to Runcorn.

For over a hundred years, the Canal was the principal route to and from Manchester for large and heavy loads, principally because of the poor condition of the main road. There were at least three wharves in Sale, situated near each bridge over the canal. Loading and unloading the barges was usually done by wheelbarrows and planks, although derricks were available at certain points for the very heavy goods. Barges transporting vegetables and fruit into Manchester returned with coal, building stone, timber, iron and night soil (the latter to be used as a fertiliser in the many market gardens around Sale and Altrincham). Several firms had their own boats on the canal, for example, in 1824 the timber firm of David Bellhouse and Co. instituted a steam boat which pulled two barges from Runcorn to Manchester. By 1850 the boat was towing thirteen barges. Goods traffic on the canal continued to grow right through the nineteeth century, as the following figures show:

Year	Tons carried
1801	334,000
1840	1,015,571
1885	c.2,000,000

Passenger traffic was also extensive especially before the opening of the railway in 1849. Merchants and solicitors travelled to their place of work in Manchester by boat, returning by the same method in the evening. Around 1800 the fare from Altrincham to Manchester was 1s. (5p) in the front cabin and 9d. (3½p) in the back cabin. The boats were pulled by two horses at a

Poor Rate Notice, July 1860. At 10d in the £, this raised £750 6s 1½d. (Reproduced by kind perimission of Trafford Local Studies Centre.)

speed of 5 or 6 mph.

When the railway from Manchester to Altrincham was opened, the canal boats running from Timperley to Manchester were withdrawn, but the packet-boats from Lymm and Runcorn to Manchester continued to run for another forty or fifty years.

Roads

The main road through the townships was originally the Roman road from Chester to Manchester. One or two writers have named it 'Holford Street' although many nineteenth-century writers sought to heighten its importance by regarding it as an extension of 'Watling Street'. At that time the road was probably bordered by waste ground on either side (see 'Sale Moor', above). The northern 600 yards of the road, from School Road to the Mersey, were named 'Cross Street', taking the name from the cross which used to mark the ford or bridge over the River Mersey. During the seventeenth and eighteenth centuries a number of houses, shops and inns were built along the road, most of them being on the Ashton side of the road. The result was a separate hamlet - 'Cross Street' - which was listed as being distinct from Ashton and Sale in directories as late as the 1860's. The southern part, from School Road to Siddall's Bridge, was 'The Washway' or 'Washway Road', because its convex construction allowed rainwater to wash dirt and rubbish into channels at each side of the road.

The road from Manchester to Stretford was turnpiked in 1750, and then fifteen years later the turnpike was extended to Altrincham. This was an attempt to improve the terrible state of the roads. Traffic had now to pay a toll to pass along the road, and the money collected paid for the upkeep of the road. Goods were carried in carts and wagons, while passenger traffic travelled in private carriages or horse omnibuses. By 1845 in addition to the long distance coaches running through Sale, there were hourly horse omnibuses to and from Manchester.

We have details of tolls at other tollgates, and these give us an idea of what might have been charged in Sale: wagons (four horses) 1/6d each, coaches (two horses) 1/-, chaises 6d, cattle ½d and sheep ¼d. The two tollgates in Sale were situated one just south of Crossford Bridge and the other near the end of Woodhouse Lane.

A list of roads in Sale dated 17th October 1812 has survived, detailing the roads which the township had to maintain at that time. These totalled 9 miles 662 yards (excluding the main road, which was maintained by the Turnpike Trust).

Churches and Parishes

The old parish of Bowdon originally included nine townships. Ashton-on-Mersey was the first new parish to be created out of Bowdon parish when St. Martin's Church in Ashton-on-Mersey was built around 1304. The

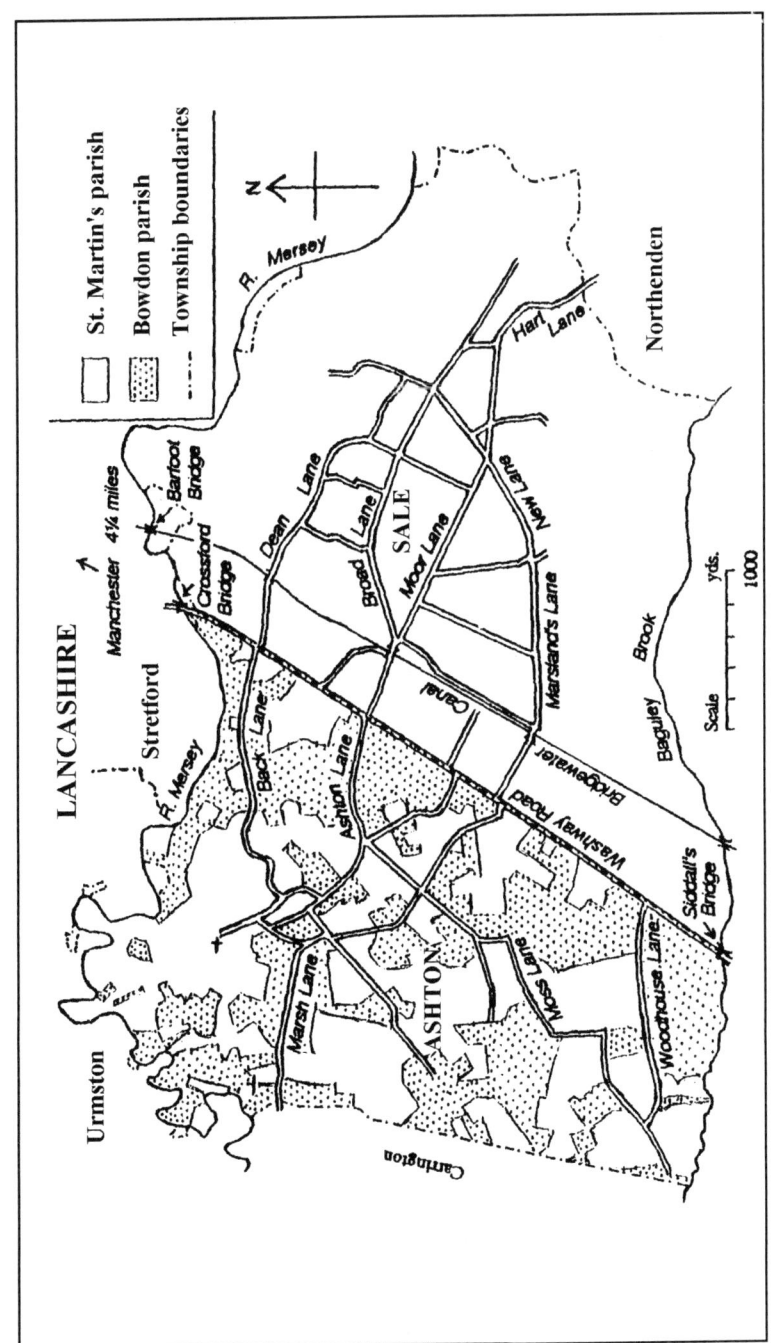

Parish boundaries in Ashton and Sale in the first half of the nineteenth century

new parish included all the township of Sale and part of Ashton-on-Mersey. For some intriguing reason, half of Ashton township was left in Bowdon parish. The division between St. Martin's and Bowdon parishes in Ashton township was like a patchwork quilt, with adjacent houses and fields belonging to different parishes (see map, p.15). This situation remained until 1893, when the Bowdon part of Ashton township was transferred to St. Martin's.

There were two non-conformist chapels in 1806. These were Cross Street Chapel and the Independent (Congregational) Chapel. Cross Street Chapel on Chapel Road was built in 1739 as a Presbyterian chapel, but the congregation gradually turned to Unitarianism. The Independent Chapel near Sale Bridge was newly opened in 1805. Although there were a number of Methodists in the area, meeting in each others' houses, the first Methodist chapel was not opened until 1820 on Broad Road.

When the parish of St. Anne's was formed as a separate entity in 1856, the whole of Sale was transferred from St. Martin's to the new parish.

Tithes

At the beginning of our period everyone had to pay a tenth of their income or produce (a 'tithe') to the church. This had been the practice for a thousand years, although over the centuries the payment had been commuted in a number of parishes to cash. The system of paying chickens, wheat and barley was very cumbersome and non-Church of England inhabitants objected to it strongly. The Tithes Commission was set up to commute the tithe payment in the remaining parishes. So that the level of payment could be fixed for each individual, large-scale maps had to be drawn up of each parish and township, with details of the owners and occupiers of every house and field. Sale's Tithe Award was dated 20th April, 1844, and the Map and Apportionment have been extremely useful in providing information for this book.

Lords of the Manor

The original Lords of the Manor were the Masseys. Over the years the title had devolved upon the Egertons of Tatton. By the beginning of the nineteenth century the title was a matter of prestige only, the Manorial Courts having long ceased to operate. Lord Egerton sold the title to John Moore in 1810, and he in turn sold it to the Worthingtons in 1840.

Local Government

For most of the period covered by this book, local government was in the hands of the Township Vestry, a meeting of the local landowners and rate-payers. Each one had a number of votes according to the size of his property, and each year they elected various officers from their number to run the township. These officers were the Overseers of the Poor (who collected the Poor Rate and distributed it to the poor), the Surveyors of the Highways (who inspected the township's roads and organised repairs), Churchwardens (who looked after the fabric of the church and its requirements for services) and the Assessors of Assessed Taxes.

Each type of officer could levy a rate, and some (e.g. the Overseers of the Poor) regularly levied two rates per year. Occasionally an extra rate was levied for an unusual occurrence, for example when money was required for the erection of a 'lock-up shop' for the Township Constable.

In 1867 Sale became a Local Government District, and from that date township affairs were run by the newly-elected Local Board, although the Township Vestry continued to exercise powers regarding the poor and Brooklands Cemetery.

The Poor

There being no State benefits, persons who could not sustain themselves financially were dependent on hand-outs from the Overseers of the Poor and, as in the case of Ashton-on-Mersey, grants from funds left as charities. Most of the hand-outs were for help with rent payments, although there were often requests for clothing and bedding. As the recipients of these hand-outs were a drain on the finances of the township, they were strongly encouraged to move elsewhere unless they could prove that they were born in the township.

House and Road Names

Until 1867, there were no house numbers in Sale and some roads had several names. All houses were known by some sort of name. Often the name of one house was applied to several others in the vicinity especially if these did not have separate names. A good example is 'Temple', which covered Temple Road, Oak Road and houses near them in Northenden Road. 'Aroma Terrace' covered two semi-detached houses and one detached house in Wardle Road, plus one detached house in Montague Road. From 1871 house numbers were applied, but these were only useful in identifying houses in the poorer streets, as the residents of larger houses preferred to use their house names. Some of the roads containing larger houses (e.g. the east side of Wardle Road) appear not to have used numbers until the 1920's. Gaps were often left in the numbering system where plots of land were not yet built on. Even so, many streets had to be renumbered at least once over the years as new houses were built, which is very confusing for modern researchers.

Road names were standardised in 1867. All the 'lanes' became 'roads', with a small number of exceptions (e.g. Baguley Lane, Gratrix Lane, Roebuck Lane and Fairy Lane). Wythenshawe Road is a good example of several names being applied to one road before 1867. In the 1841 census it is regarded as part of 'Dane Lane', in the 1857 rate book it is part of 'Broad Lane', in the 1861 census it is 'Northen Lane' and in the 1861 rate book it is 'Dane Lane' again.

Although most of the large houses have been demolished, the stone gateposts survive in many cases - especially on Brooklands Road and Wardle Road.

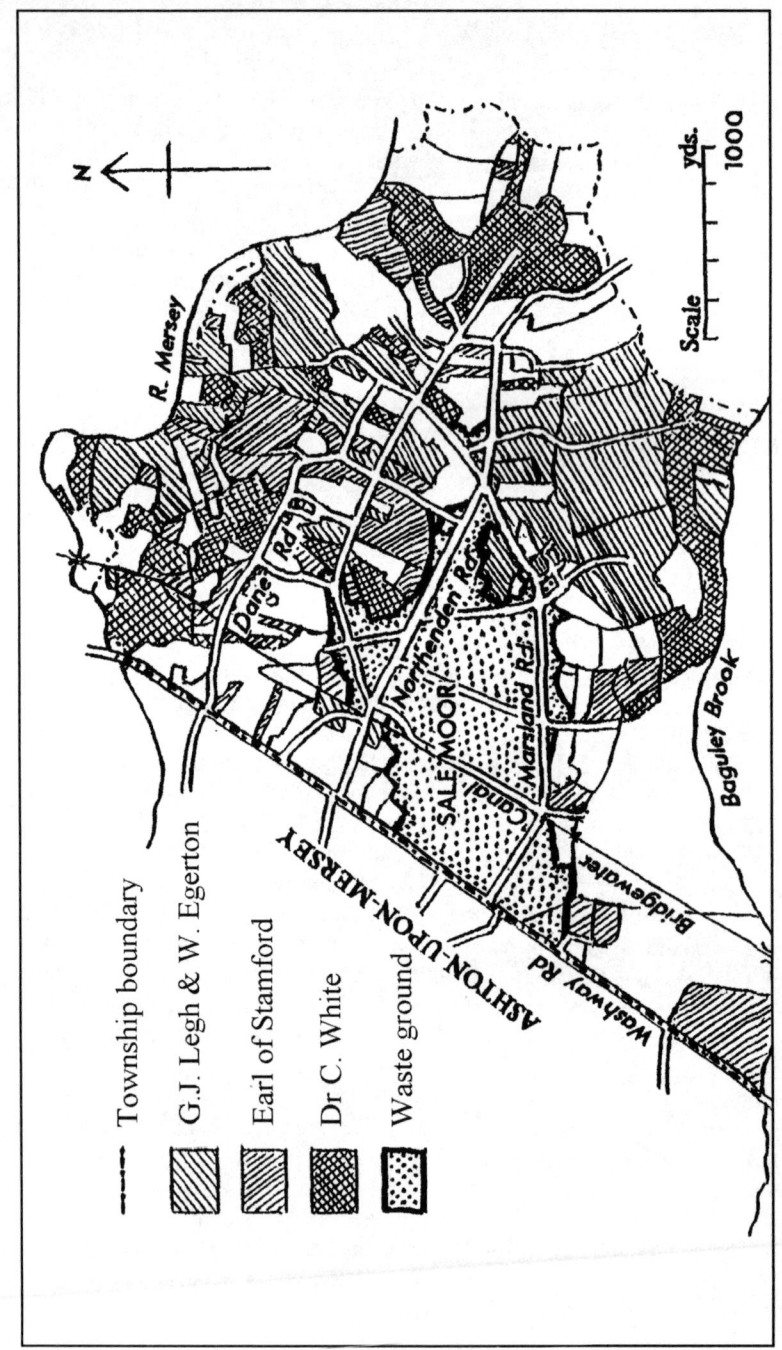

Land ownership in Sale in 1806

2. LAND & PROPERTY OWNERSHIP

Land Ownership

In most townships the principal detailed account of nineteenth-century ownership of land and property is the Tithe Schedule. We are very lucky that, in the case of Sale, we also have the Enclosure Maps of 1806-7, with schedules almost as detailed as those of the Tithe Award. This means that it is possible to see exactly how the ownership of farms, fields and dwellings changed over the thirty-eight years from 1806 to 1844.

	1806	1844
Cultivated land	1604 acres	1911 acres
Waste land, roads and water	321	70
Total	1925	1981
No. of owners (incl. lessees)	51	97 (6)
No. of occupiers	76	128

Notes

(i) The reason for the difference of 56 acres in total area is obscure, as the boundaries of the township remained unchanged.
(ii) The differences in 'Cultivated land' and 'Waste land, roads and water' between 1806 and 1844 are explained by the fact that 279 acres of waste land (Sale Moor) were enclosed in 1807, although again the figures do not balance exactly.
(iii) The above figures for the number of owners include 'lessees' (shown in brackets).
(iv) The numbers of occupiers may not be absolutely accurate, as one person was sometimes listed as 'occupying' two separate houses, when he or she obviously sub-let one to tenants. The existence of a number of people with identical names also introduces an element of uncertainty. Not only did many sons have the same Christian name as their fathers, but families with the same surname tended to use the same Christian names. For example, in 1806 there were four families in Sale with the surname 'Marsland'. Each family had members named Robert, Edward, James, Betty and Mary.

The following is a break-down of the properties owned, according to size:

	1806	1844
Under 1 acre	10	20
1-5 acres	15	20
6-9 acres	5	15
10-19 acres	5	10

19

20-29 acres	4	7
30-39 acres	6	5
40-49 acres	1	7
50-99 acres	1	4
100 acres and over	4	4

From the above tables we see to what extent the Manor of Sale had become fragmented by 1806 and how this continued through the first half of the nineteenth century. The numbers of properties with less than 20 acres rose from 35 in 1806 to 65 in 1844. This fragmentation was greatly accelerated after the building of the railway in 1849, which in effect quickly converted Sale and Ashton from agricultural communities into dormitory suburbs of Manchester. We have no detailed figures of the areas of land owned after 1844, but the Rate Books give us the names of owners and occupiers. By 1860 the number of 'owners' had increased to 208 and that of 'occupiers' to 612; by 1876 these figures were 437 and 1416 respectively. By the latter date, the names of the large landowners of the early nineteenth century had disappeared completely from the lists - all their land had been sold off, mostly for housing.

The chief landowners in the first half of the nineteenth century were:

	1806	**1844**
Legh & Egerton families	356 acres	181 acres
Lord Stamford	265	-
White family	256	291
Lawrence Wright	135	154
Samuel Brooks	-	166
Mrs. Woodiwiss	-	100

The Manor of Sale was divided into two parts some time before 1187 AD. Half was held by the Massey family for over five hundred years, and when the male line died out their share was handed down the female line until in 1785 part of the estate was bequeathed to the Leghs of High Legh. Thus in 1806 George John Legh (1768-1832) of East Legh Hall, High Legh, was the largest landowner in Sale. Another part of the Massey estate had been purchased by the Egertons of Tatton Hall near Knutsford. According to the Enclosure Schedule of 1806-7 George John Legh owned 202 acres jointly with Wilbraham Egerton (1781-1856). This included Sale Old Hall and Lime Tree Farm, the second largest farm in Sale. By 1807 all this property had been sold (see further detail on pp.121-24). In addition to the above joint holding George John Legh himself owned 154 acres, which included farms on Chapel Road, Broad Road, Baguley Road, Dane Road and two at Moor Nook.

Lord Stamford lived in Dunham Massey Hall. His land came from the other half of the Manor of Sale, part of which the Booth family acquired by purchase in 1604. Their land in 1806 included Washway Farm, Whitehall Farm and other farms on Broad Road and north of Dane Road. By 1830 all had been disposed of. Three of the farms (112 acres) were sold to various owners and the rest of the estate (153 acres) was sold to Samuel Brooks (1793-1864), the Manchester banker.

Dr. Charles White's grandfather came from Nottinghamshire and settled in Manchester towards the end of the seventeenth century. Some thirty years later the family bought land in Sale from the descendants of the Masseys and about 1711 built 'Sale Priory'. In 1806 Dr. White owned 'Sale Priory' and much of the land between the 'Priory' and the Bridgewater Canal; he also owned Sale New Hall, Chadwick's Farm and Wallbank Farm, a total of 256 acres. Although Chadwick's Farm was sold in 1809 (see below), over the next twenty years the Whites' overall acreage increased by the purchase of 100 acres from other owners. Much of this consisted of woods and copses.

There were 40 farms of at least 10 acres in 1806. Their sizes were:

10-19 acres	9 farms
20-29 acres	15
30-39 acres	6
40-49 acres	2
50-99 acres	6
100 acres and over	2

Thus we see that 75% of the farms were between 10 and 39 acres in size. During the period 1806-1844 at least seven of the smaller (20-acre) farms disappeared, as they were sold and their fields were incorporated into other farms. Perhaps the most striking example of this is that of 'Waterside'. There were two farms in the north-east corner of Sale, near the River Mersey - 'Waterside Farm', owned by William Whitelegg, and 'Waterside', owned by Thomas Hesketh. The latter consisted of a farmhouse and 11 fields round it. Thirty-eight years later all that remained was the farmhouse, which was now the home of a labourer and his family. Not only had the fields been sold to two different owners, but the majority of the fields had disappeared altogether, being amalgamated with others to form the largest field in Sale. The new field covered 34 acres and was appropriately named 'Great Meadow'.

House Ownerhip

In addition to normal house ownership, building houses was a method of investing one's profits, when banks were few and far between. Several shop-keepers and artisans owned a number of houses, from which they drew rents. Examples of these are Thomas Johnson, Thomas Lamb, Luke Winstanley, George Bloor and Thomas Brickell.

On the other hand, there was a tendency for the professional classes in the largest houses not to own their houses but to rent them. Examples of this are

William Joynson (who rented 'Ashfield' for thirty years before finally buying it), John Brogden, David Bellhouse, and the successive residents of 'Woodheys' and the 'Priory'.

There was one unusual custom regarding house ownership which is worthy of mention. There are a number of cases where a person owned one house, but let it out, while they themselves lived in a smaller rented property. While one or two instances of this may be expected, it seems in fact to have been almost the norm. Possibly the larger rent covered the owner's smaller outgoings and also left him with a little extra income.

3. POPULATION & OCCUPATIONS

Population
The annual Census Summaries give the following figures:

Year	Population of Ashton	Population of Sale	No. of houses in Sale
1801	778	819	136
1811	918	901	160
1821	875	1049	?
1831	974	1104	200
1841	1105	1309	254
1851	1174	1720	375
1861	1476	3031	597
1871	2359	5573	1114
1881	3326	7915	1503

The 1840's saw the beginning of the flight of the well-to-do out of Manchester to the suburbs. We see that they preferred Sale to Ashton, principally because of the attraction of the railway. In 1801 Sale's population was only 5% greater than that of Ashton; eighty years later it was 235% greater.

In the forty years between 1801 and 1841 Sale's population increased by 60%; in the forty years between 1841 and 1881 it increased by 605%.

One other figure which is interesting is the decrease in the size of families. In 1801 there were 819 people and 136 families; in 1841, 1309 people and 253 families and in 1881, 7915 people and 1608 families. These give the following average sizes for a family:

1801	6.0 people
1841	5.2
1881	4.9

These figures are slightly inflated because the total population figures include people who are not part of a family (e.g. lodgers, servants, etc.), but the underlying trend must be correct.

Another interesting figure is the percentage of females in the total population.

1801	431 males	388 females	819 total
1841	638	671	1309
1881	3393	4522	7915

In 1801 there were 11% more males than females; eighty years later there were 33% more females than males. One of the main reasons for this must be the influx of professional people, each family bringing with them a number of female servants.

Occupations

We do not have detailed figures of occupations in the early part of the nineteenth century. The only information we have is that given in the Census Summaries.

The 1801 Census Summary says of the 819 inhabitants of Sale, 479 (58%) worked in agriculture, 332 (41%) in 'manufacturing' and 8 (1%) in 'other'. As these figures add up to the total population, they must include wives, children and servants. They must therefore be based on families, and this was also the basis for the figures of the 1811 Census Summary. 'Manufacturing' presumably includes tradesmen (blacksmiths, wheelwrights, weavers, shoemakers, etc.), shop-keepers and possibly 'other miscellaneous' (see below).

When we come to the 1841 census, we have much more information. A detailed analysis of occupations is given in *Sale, Cheshire, in 1841*. In order to provide a meaningful comparison with both 1801 and 1871, I have reduced the occupations to five headings. These are 'agriculture', 'tradesmen & retailers', 'other miscellaneous (e.g. boatmen, charwomen, coachmen), 'professional' and 'other independent' (people with private means). As in the 1801 Census Summary, the figures are now based on heads of families rather than individuals.

	1801	1841	1871
agriculture	58%	50%	16%
trades & retailers ⎤	41%	21%	22%
misc. Other ⎦		14%	25%
Professional ⎤	1%	4%	28%
other independent ⎦		11%	9%

These figures show extremely clearly the transition of Sale from agriculture to dormitory town. The number of farm workers and gardeners decreased from 58% in 1801 to 50% in 1841 and to 16% in 1871. The largest group in 1871 is that of professional people, most of whom worked not in Sale but in Manchester.

Domestic servants are not included in the above figures. In 1841 10% of the total population of Sale worked in domestic service. Thirty years later this figure was almost the same - 9.5%.

In 1841 16.5% of the population of Sale were born outside Cheshire (further details of birthplace were not given in this census). In 1871 this figure had risen to 58.4%. Many of these were born in Manchester and had moved to the

Cheshire countryside, but there were also people from almost every English county (especially from Yorkshire) and Scotland, Wales and Ireland (the latter is particularly well represented). Sale was now becoming quite cosmopolitan. Other birthplaces further afield included Germany, U.S.A, Canada, Mexico, Brazil, Belgium, Bulgaria, Poland, Russia, Italy, Switzerland, Norway, Sweden, Czechoslovakia, Syria and Australia.

Three of the men mentioned in this book are prime examples of the possibility of upward mobility in the nineteenth century. John Brogden was originally a butcher and horse dealer, but later built railways all over Britain, on the Continent and also in New Zealand. David Bellhouse's father was a humble joiner who built up possibly the largest firm of builders and contractors in Britain. Some of David's children married into the professional classes. Samuel Brooks's father was handloom manufacturer. Samuel became a banker and property owner, and when he died in 1864 his estate was worth more than two million pounds. His son, William Cunliffe Brooks, was knighted and married into the aristocracy. There must be many more examples of this on a smaller scale.

4. EVENTS

Main events in the township 1806-76

1807	Sale Moor enclosed (see p.11).
1808	Ashton & Sale Volunteer Militia disbanded.
1810	John Moore bought the Manor of Sale from Wilbraham Egerton & George J. Legh.
1811 (26th May)	Colours of Ashton & Sale Volunteers laid in St. Martin's Church.
1821	Select Vestry set up to handle the concerns of the poor.
1835 (April)	Rev. R. Popplewell Johnson died; succeeded by Rev C. Backhouse Sowerby.
1836	Ashton-upon-Mersey & Sale joined the Altrincham Poor Law Union, but relief of the poor continued on a township basis.
1840 (March)	Communion plate stolen from St. Martin's Church.
	The Worthingtons bought Sale Old Hall and the Manor of Sale from John Moore.
1849 (20th July)	Manchester, South Junction & Altrincham Railway opened from Oxford Road (Manchester) to Altrincham (see p.27).
1856	Whole of Sale Township transferred from St. Martin's to new St. Anne's parish.
1859	William Wilson requested to produce an up-to date map and reference book.
1860	Stretford Gas Co. and North Cheshire Water began to supply Sale.
1862	Brooklands Cemetery opened.
1866	St. Anne's became a civil parish.
(May)	Rev. C.B. Sowerby retired; Rev. Joseph Ray became rector.
	Town Vestry voted against adopting Local Government Act of 1858; poll of inhabitants said 'yes'.
1867 (19th Feb.)	Sale became a Local Government District; the Board consisted of William Joynson (chairman), Alfred Watkin, Isaac Hoyle, John Storey, William Wilson, Joseph Cordingley, William Butterfield, James Hodgson, John Morley, William Thornber and James Worthington. The powers of the Township Vestry were now very much reduced.
1875	First street-lighting in Sale (45 gas lamps).
(Sept.)	'Oaklands' purchased for Local Board Offices.

(Sept.)   'Oaklands' purchased for Local Board Offices.
1876   Ambulance to be bought for the township.
                  Lamplighters appointed.
                  Brooklands Cemetery extended.

Main national events 1806-76

1807	Abolition of slave trade in British Empire.
1812 (May)	Spencer Percival (British Prime Minister) assassinated
1815 (18th June)	Battle of Waterloo. Napoleon finally defeated. Income tax abolished.
1819 (16th Aug.)	Peterloo Massacre in Manchester.
1820 (Jan.)	George IV became king.
1829	Catholic Emancipation Act. Catholics free to take office. Britain's first official police force established.
1830 (June)	William IV became king.
(15th Sept.)	Manchester to Liverpool Railway opened.
1832	First Reform Bill. More property-owners allowed to vote.
1833	First Factory Act. Some restrictions on employment of children & women.
1834	Poor Law Amendment Act. Workhouses & Poor Law Unions set up.
1837 (June)	Queen Victoria became queen.
1840	Penny post instituted.
1844	Second Factory Act. Further restrictions on employment of children & women.
1846	Repeal of the Corn Laws. Restrictions on importing corn removed (price of bread reduced).
1851	Great Exhibition in Hyde Park (London) and at Old Trafford.
1854-6	Crimean War. Britain & France v. Russia.
1862	Cotton famine in Lancashire.
1867	Second Reform Bill. Number of voters doubled. Still based on value of property owned.
1870	Education Act: local school boards instituted; education for all children, but not free for all.
1871	Trades Unions legalised.
1872	Secret ballot introduced in Britain.

The Railway (1849)

The Manchester, South Junction and Altrincham Railway was promoted in 1845 as a 1-mile line to link London Road (later 'Piccadilly') and Victoria stations in Manchester, with a 7½-mile branch from Knott Mill to Altrincham. It was promoted by two separate railway companies, who were often deadly rivals. These were the London and North Western Railway and the Manchester, Sheffield & Lincolnshire Railway. As the chairmanship at board meetings of the MSJ&AR alternated between the two railways, decisions taken at one meeting were often rescinded at the next meeting. The joint ownership continued under different names right through to nationalisation in 1947.

The branch to Altrincham soon became the most important part of the system. The first trains ran from Oxford Road station (Manchester) to Altrincham Old Station on Friday, the 20th July, 1849. The last ½ mile to the 'Bowdon' terminus (actually on Lloyd Street, Altrincham) was opened six weeks later. Sale Bridge over the Bridgewater Canal was widened to accommodate the railway, and Sale station was built on the bridge. From 1856 to 1883 Sale station was called 'Sale and Sale Moor' (referring to the area immediately east of the line rather than the modern 'village' at the junction of Marsland Road and Northenden Road). In December 1859 a second Sale station was opened at Marsland's Bridge. This was the result of pressure from the inhabitants of the area and also of a promise from Samuel Brooks (the Manchester banker and local landowner) that if the receipts from this station did not exceed £100 within five years, he would personally pay the railway £300. In fact the receipts reached £100 in less than two years. Brooks insisted that the new station be called 'Brooklands'.

At a Township Vestry meeting held in December 1844 the Vestry members passed a resolution that 'the proposed railway ... will be very prejudicial and injurious to property, roads and the public highway in the Township'. One of the signatories was John Brogden, who nine months later submitted a successful tender for building the branch to Altrincham. Both the contractors who built the line lived in Sale. The line from London Road to Ordsall Lane was built by David Bellhouse & Sons; David Bellhouse lived at 'Sale Heys Cottage'. This part of the line was all on viaduct, and consisted of 224 arches which required 50 million bricks. The branch to Altrincham was longer but easier to build. There was only one tunnel (at Trafford Bar) and a section of viaduct near Castlefield. From Stretford to Timperley the line ran alongside the Bridgewater Canal. The total cost of the railway was £575,000.

In 1854 the branch became a through route, when the Warrington & Stockport Railway was allowed to run its trains over it from Timperley Junction to Manchester. The following year saw Great Western Railway trains running along the line on their way from Shrewsbury to Manchester, and in 1858 the Great Northern and Manchester, Sheffield and Lincolnshire Railways started running over the line from Piccadilly to Timperley Junction as part of their route to Liverpool. Another railway which ran trains over the line was the Cheshire Lines Committee (from 1862 to Knutsford, from 1864 to 1873 to Liverpool, and from 1874 to Chester).

Although passenger traffic on the railway was light at first, it soon began to grow, especially as the number of inhabitants in the each of the various towns along the route rapidly increased. By the 1880's the line was one of the busiest

28

commuter routes in the north-west. It was electrified in 1931 and since 15th June, 1992, has operated as the southern half of the Metrolink Light Rapid Transit System.

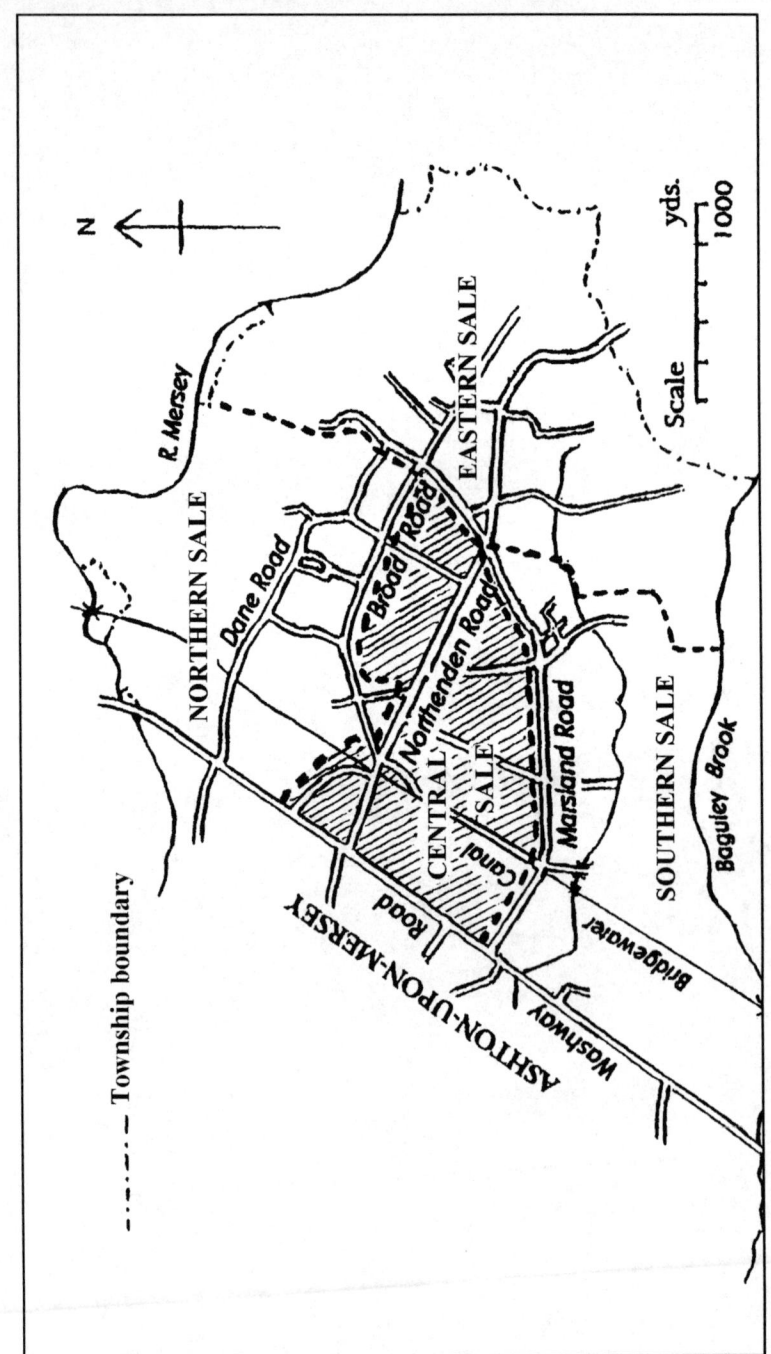

Sale divided into four areas for the purpose of this book.

5. THE DEVELOPMENT OF CENTRAL SALE 1806-1876

The area covered by this section is bounded by Chapel Road and Broad Road in the north, Cross Street and Washway Road in the west, Marsland Road in the south, and Old Hall Road in the east. In general it covers the area within these roads (see map, p.30). Broad Road itself is dealt with in section 5 ('Northern Sale'), Marsland Road is dealt with in section 6 ('Southern Sale'), and Old Hall Road is dealt with in section 7 ('Eastern Sale'). The present section covers all School Road, and Northenden Road as far as the Legh Arms; it also describes the various roads leading from these (e.g Hereford Street, Hope Road, Wardle Road, Derbyshire Road, Irlam Road, Temple Road, etc.)

The Area in 1806

The only cultivated areas in central Sale in 1806 were (i) both sides of School Road and (ii) most of the area between Northenden Road and Broad Road. The rest of the area covered by this chapter was waste land - 'Sale Moor' (see p.11)

(i) Cross Street

This section deals with the part of Cross Street between School Road and Chapel Road (the northern part of Cross Street is described in section 5). Cross Street was part of the Roman road from Chester to Manchester, and took its name from the cross which marked the ford or ferry over the River Mersey.

School Road joined Cross Street at a narrow junction. On the north-east corner stood the 'Bull's Head', which was owned by John Royle and leased by William Whitelegg (*1766-1824). Next to the inn stood a row of six cottages. These were owned by William Whitelegg, and the occupants included his mother, Nancy (*1740-1811). Further along there were two pairs of cottages. The first pair belonged to one of the occupants, Richard Pearson; the second pair was owned by Joseph Atkinson (the names of the occupants are not known). Joseph Atkinson (1752-1818) lived in 'Ashfield', a large house which stood in its own 2½ acres of ground near the junction of Cross Street and Chapel Road. Joseph, who was born in Manchester, was a hat-manufacturer and had formerly lived near his factory in Cupid's Alley, off Deansgate (Manchester). In 1793 he bought 'Ashfield' and the surrounding land from Richard Irlam Grantham, a descendant of the Irlam family who had owned the house and neighbouring land in the eighteenth century. Ten years later Joseph moved to Sale with his wife, Elizabeth, although he maintained a house in Cupid's Alley. The latter was later named 'Atkinson Street' in his honour. He also owned land in Ashton-on Mersey, and forty years after his death one of the new roads through this land was named 'Atkinson Road'.

(ii) Chapel Road

In 1739 the Presbyterians built a new chapel on land donated by Benjamin Irlam; the chapel was always known as 'Cross Street Chapel' although it was 75 yards from Cross Street itself. The road on which it was situated was originally 'Bythell's Lane', but soon became known as 'Chapel Lane'. By 1770 the congregation had become Unitarian in belief, and in 1777 the Rev. Robert Harrop of Hale Unitarian Chapel was invited to take Cross Street Chapel under his wing. He continued as pastor of both chapels until his death in 1813. Apart from the chapel, the only other buildings on the south side of the road were four cottages which faced the canal just behind the new Independent Chapel. These were owned by Peter Hulme, one of the occupants, who probably worked on the canal side, loading and unloading barges.

On the north side of Chapel Road there were two buildings. One, opposite Cross Street Chapel, was a cottage rented from Joseph Atkinson by Thomas Haslam; it probably housed some of his farm labourers. The other, nearer the canal, was a farm leased from G.J. Legh by William Morris. The farm covered 10 acres and included three fields behind the township school in School Road.

(iii) School Road

We do not know when School Road (or 'School Lane', as it was called until 1867) came into being. It possibly dates from the mid-1600's. It was certainly important enough in 1766 for a bridge to be built over the canal at this point. The bridge was very narrow - 12 or 13 feet wide at the most (the modern bridge over the canal and railway is five times as wide).

Both sides of School Road had been enclosed by 1806, as was the area between School Road and Chapel Road. This meant that the area now consisted of fields surrounded by hedges, and most of it was the property of Joseph Atkinson (see above). Early in the nineteenth century it was possible to see northwards as far as the Mersey and southwards over the Moor to Raglan Road.

Along the whole of School Road there were only six buildings in 1806. Two of them were on the north side. Timothy Richardson (*1758-1829) and his wife, Sarah, lived in a house and garden situated opposite the present-day Hayfield Street; the other building was the new Independent Chapel near the canal. This had been built during the previous year on a site now occupied by Sale Civic Theatre at a total cost of £600.

The south side of School Road had four buildings along it. Two houses near the junction of School Road and Washway Road were the property of John Royle, who also owned the 'Bull's Head' opposite. One of these was rented by George Oldfield (*1749-1823), a blacksmith living with his first wife Ann. Next to the cottages was the home of John Heywood (Howard) (*1766-1851); fields then extended as far as the new Township School which had been built about six years earlier. The school was situated halfway between the modern shopping mall and Springfield Road. It was a spartan affair with stone floors

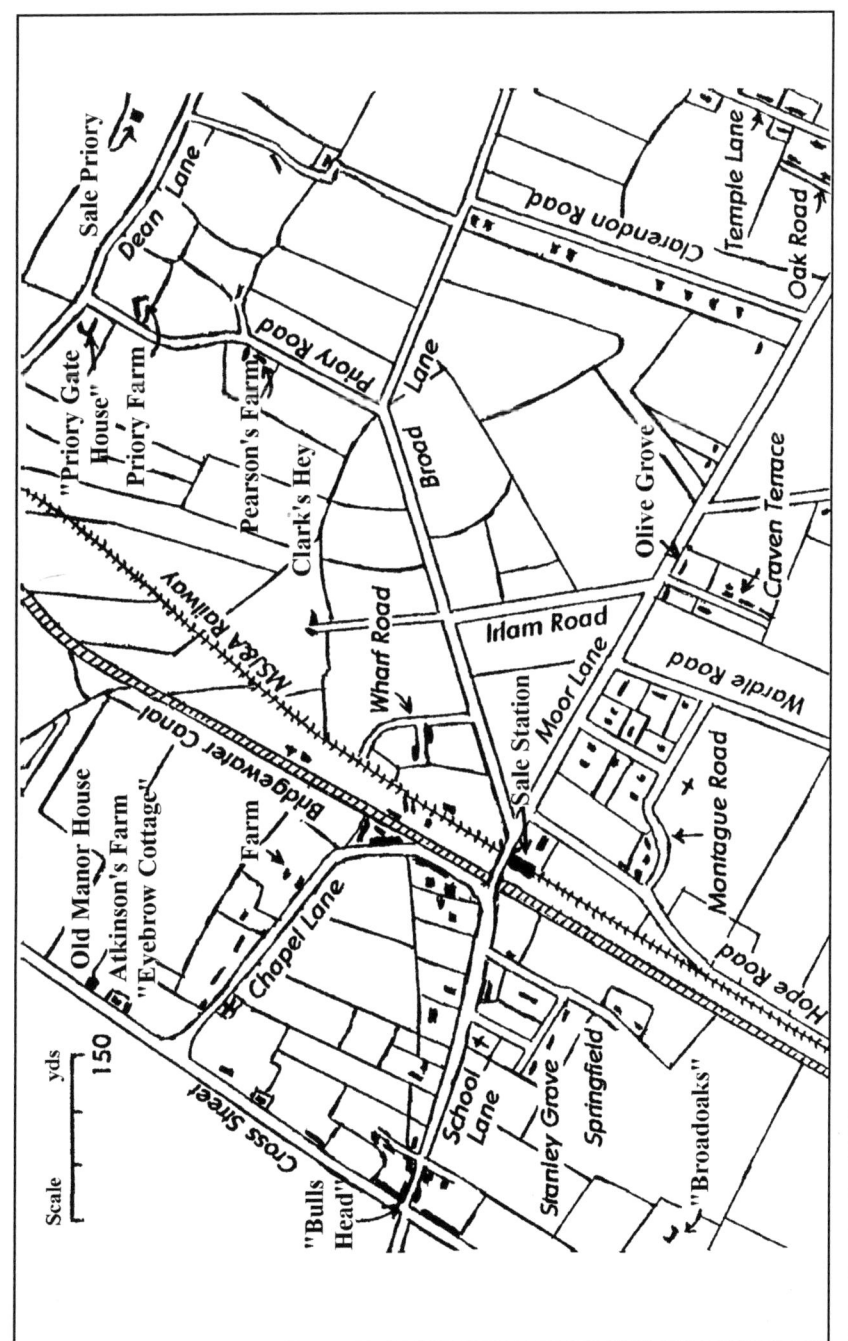

Sale Centre in 1860

and very little heating, but it lasted until 1879, when another school was built at the corner of Springfield Road. The last building on the south side was the former school-house, set back from the road; this was now a cottage.

(iv) Northenden Road

The earliest route from Ashton-upon-Mersey to Northenden was via Glebelands Road and Dane Road. Probably by 1650 A.D. a more direct route was available by way of Ashton Lane and School Road. From the bridge over the canal this route ran in a straight line through the northern area of Sale Moor to a junction with Marsland Road, near the Legh Arms. The road was understandably called 'Moor Lane' until it was renamed in 1867, along with most of Sale's roads. In 1806 the land on either side was not enclosed by hedges, but was uncultivated ground. Because of this, there were very few buildings to be seen. Having crossed the canal by means of Sale Bridge, a traveller would see rough grassland extending in front as far as the eye could see, to the right beyond Marsland Road, and to left as far as the River Mersey.

Two straight roads ran southwards across the Moor, from Northenden Road to Marsland Road. These were (i) 'Moss's Lane', which led to Whitehall Farm and later became 'Wardle Road' and (ii) the road to 'Higson's corner', which later became 'Derbyshire Road'. These two roads were relatively new in 1806, and were not bounded by hedges, as all the older roads were.

On the north side of Northenden Road there were three properties. The first was a small farm of four acres situated at the end of the modern Holly Grove on a site now occupied by Norfolk House. It was rented from the Earl of Stamford by Thomas Alderley (*1772-1830), the oldest son of William Alderley of Wallbank Farm. The next property, at the junction with Temple Road, was a row of cottages called 'The Temple'. The origin of this name has not yet been discovered; it was possibly ironic, as the occupants seem to have been agricultural labourers of various kinds. Near the junction with Marsland Road a farmhouse stood back from the road. This was the home of Robert Barlow (*1748-1820) and his wife Martha. Together they farmed 8 acres around their house.

The only buildings on the south side were situated immediately over the canal bridge, on the site of the later 'Queen's Hotel' (now 'The Station at Sale'). These buildings formed the home of James Hope (*1754-1811), who gave his name to a third road which ran along the canal from Northenden Road, past his house, to Marsland's Bridge.

Right on the canal bank itself there was a house and croft belonging to Martha Royle. It seems reasonable to assume from the position of her house that she undertook some work connected with the canal itself.

(v) Temple Road

The northern section of Temple Road was called 'Finch Lane' until 1867. There were no buildings in 1806 between Northenden Road and Broad Road.

(vi) Washway Road

This chapter covers the portion of Washway Road between School Road and Marsland Road. The southern two thirds, roughly from the modern Sibson Road to Marsland Road, was bordered by Sale Moor (see p.11), and this was where the Duke of Gloucester reviewed the local troops and volunteers in April 1804. There were, however, two houses at the corner of School Road and Washway Road, next to George Oldfield's house in School Road; these were rented from Joseph Atkinson by Thomas Massey and a Miss Siddall. 30 yards south of where the modern Sibson Road meets Washway Road stood the home of John Royle (the owner of the 'Bull's Head' and other properties in School Road). Further down, a track ran from Washway Road to the canal, possibly leading to some sort of wharf. This track later became Roebuck Lane.

1806-1841

The Enclosure Award of 1807 had a far-reaching effect on Sale. The waste land known as 'Sale Moor' was parcelled out among the existing land-owners roughly in proportion to their current holding (see p.12). These parcels of land now became fields which were enclosed by hedges. Although the central area was transformed as crops were planted, the number of new houses built between 1806 and 1841 was extremely small.

(i) Cross Street

The owner of 'Ashfield', Joseph Atkinson, died suddenly in the middle of a service at the Friends' Meeting House on South Street, Manchester, on New Year's Day, 1818. His widow, Elizabeth, died of shock 24 days later. Their son, Thomas (1791-1867), was not as successful in business as his father, and appears to have had to move away and rent the Sale property out to various businessmen from 1820 onwards (see p.145). At the time of the 1841 census 'Ashfield' was unoccupied.

When William Whitelegg died in 1824 the running of the 'Bull's Head' was taken over by his brother, James (*1774-1838). Later the tenancy was given to George Brownhill, and then in 1839 to Peter Shawcross Tyrer (*1808-1855), who was also a butcher, a trade he had learned from his father, who lived near the 'Legh Arms'.

(ii) Chapel Road

Abraham Hewitt took over the tenancy of Chapel Lane Farm sometime between 1831 and 1836. He was born in Northenden in *1801, and lived with his first wife, Anne. He also owned a row of seven cottages which had been built near the canal. Although their official name was 'Sale Cottages', they were usually referred to by their nickname - 'Cabbage Row' (did this name reflect the staple diet of the residents?).

(iii) School Road

George Oldfield's wife died in 1809; he soon re-married and in 1812 he and his second wife Sarah moved from School Road to another smithy, at the junction of Marsland Road and Northenden Road (see p.123).

Two houses were built on the north side of School Road; these were William Alderley's house (built in 1827 next to the Independent Chapel), and 'Oak Place' (a pair of semi-detached houses set back from the road and built in 1837 for Thomas Leeds). William Alderley (*1775-1854) was a corn dealer and one of the sons of William of Wallbank Farm.

Timothy Richardson left School Road in 1822; presumably he went to live with his son Thomas at Atkinson's Farm on Cross Street. The house in School Road was then rented by Edward Dickinson (*1784-1838). The 1841 census shows that it had possibly been enlarged. It was now the home of Thomas

Cookson, Sarah Dickinson (Edward's widow) and Isaac Bythell (*1791-1864, an agricultural labourer). The houses survive as a low row of shops between Partington Place and Orchard Place.

In 1810 the schoolmaster in the Township School was Joseph Heap. He was succeeded by William Sadler, who was 'ejected' from the school in 1818 (the reason for this is not known). The Rev. John Hunter was then appointed. Born in Eccles in *1793, he had come to Ashton in 1815 as curate to the Rev Sowerby. In 1822 he married Sarah Stelfox, the heiress of the Williamson estate. When he resigned in 1836, James Warren was appointed. Born in Baguley, he was 31-years old at the time, living with his wife, Ann. The cottage which had been the old schoolhouse was now the home of James Lightfoot (1806-82), a gardener born in Sale. The Sale School Board still owned the cottage.

(iv) Northenden Road, Wardle Road & Derbyshire Road

In 1839 James Clark built three cottages on the site of the 'Temple' (the existing building was presumably demolished). The inhabitants in 1841 were three agricultural labourers - Edward Hampson, John Brownhill and William Brown - plus a blacksmith, Thomas Scelland. The 1841 census also shows that Martha Royle's house on the canal bank was now occupied by Elizabeth Atkinson, an 'oil merchant'. Another house had been recently built nearby - this was the home of William Chapman, a gardener.

When Robert Barlow died in 1820, one of his daughters, Martha, continued for some time to run the small-holding near the junction with Marsland Road. From 1831 to around 1845, however, she had help in the shape of John Kelsall (*1781-1854) and his family. Thomas Alderley's small farm was taken over by William Woodall in 1825. Three years later he bought it from Lord Stamford and in 1841 it was the home of his son, James (b. *1783), who also ran the Barlow smallholding from 1845.

After the enclosures of 1807 over twenty years passed before a few houses were built on the land which had been Sale Moor. Buildings dating from around 1832-5 were John Darbyshire's cottage on Derbyshire Road (this was later enlarged into three cottages which are still lived in today), the farm rented by Peter Wardle (*1787-1854) on the road named after him, and Edward Marsland's cottage on Northenden Road. John Darbyshire (*1774-1844), a hay dealer, was probably well-known and it seems that his name was given to the road when the new road names were introduced in 1867. One other house was built about the same time. Edward Marsland of Wright's Farm (later 'Brooklands Farm') died in 1818; he was succeeded by his son, Robert (1797-1867), who built a house for his mother, Ann, on the corner of Wardle Road and Marsland Road. The house later became a shop, and is now a garage.

Three new buildings were also erected near the junction of Marsland Road and Northenden Road. It seems that between 1831 and 1836 the 'Legh Arms' became purely a public house (run by Thomas Brickell, see p.123) and Wil-

The four houses of 'Lime Place', at the corner of Wardle Road and Northenden Road, were built in 1848-49 for the Revd. Edward Morris (see p.44).

liam Oldfield (George's son) built a smithy across the road. The other two buildings were a pair of cottages (1837) owned by Ann Marsland and 'Beech Cottage' (1840, owned by John Harrison). At the same time as the latter was built, a house was built adjoining the smithy for Thomas Scelland (*1795-1870), the blacksmith who rented the smithy.

(v) Temple Road
There were no new houses built on Temple Road during this period.

(vi) Washway Road
A terrace of eight houses was built on Washway Road in 1816; the terrace was named 'New Chester'. The inhabitants were mostly agricultural labourers; there was however one grocer's shop, which also sold beer. Twenty years later a Manchester grocer, Samuel Roebuck, bought 10 acres of land at the corner of the track leading to the canal, and in 1837 built a house there. The house - 'Sale Bank' - stood in its own grounds and was surrounded by shrubs and trees. The 1841 census shows Samuel Roebuck living with his wife, Hannah, two children, his father-in-law and five servants. Samuel (*1797-1865) was partner in the firm of Richardson & Roebuck, with premises in Market Street and Deansgate. Another house was built on the south of the track in 1839; this was 'Roseville Cottage', a pair of semi-detached houses owned by William Renshaw of Ashton. It was the home of Jeremiah Renshaw (*1810-1862, a surgeon, born in Altrincham) and James Bythell (a farmer, born in *1775). In 1841 Jeremiah Renshaw moved across the road to a house in Ashton, and his place at 'Roseville Cottage' was taken by another doctor, Henry Ollier (*1799-1852). Three cottages were also built nearer to the canal, the homes of Peter Royle, William Royle and Joseph Burgess. The track later became 'Roebuck Lane', taking its name from Samuel Roebuck.

Another terrace of eight houses ('Sale Terrace') was built in 1839 at the junction with Marsland Road. These were a better class of house than those at 'New Chester'. In 1841 only four were occupied - by a solicitor, a painter/decorator, and two ladies of independent means. 'Sale Terrace' was demolished in the 1970's and an office block built on the site.

1841-1861

The area and its inhabitants in 1841 are described in detail in *Sale, Cheshire, in 1841*, pages 24-25, 29-31 and 59-65.

The opening of the railway from Manchester to Altrincham in July 1849 (see p.27) had a profound impact on Sale and Ashton; its impact was felt most of all in central Sale. Within a few years of the coming of the railway the 'centre' of Sale had moved from Sale Green to School Road, and slowly the area we now regard as 'central Sale' was transformed from agricultural land into rows of houses. The Rev. Edward Morris of the Independent Chapel near Sale Bridge was one of the first to see the potential benefits of owning property near the railway. Before the line was opened he bought a plot of land at the corner of Wardle Road and Northenden Road (see below). Several other people bought land for housing soon after the railway opened, and by 1850 new houses were under construction or had been completed in Chapel Road, School Road, Stanley Grove, and Northenden Road. A year later houses were being built further down Northenden Road, in Clarendon Road. Yet in 1861 the area was still predominantly fields as it had been fifty years earlier.

(i) Cross Street

NB - 'Cross Street' currently starts at School Road and runs north, while 'Washway Road' runs south from the same point. In the 1850's and 1860's the distinction between them was not so clear, and properties between School Road and Sibson Road are often described in directories and censuses as being on 'Cross Street'.

There was very little change on Cross Street during the years 1841-1861. After being empty for a couple of years, 'Ashfield' gained a new tenant at the beginning of 1843. He was William Joynson (*1801-1882), a solicitor with an office in Marsden Street, Manchester. He was also a director of Peter Joynson & Co, silk manufacturers (surely an unusual combination!). He was born in Manchester and in 1851 we find him living in 'Ashfield' with his wife, Anne, four children and three servants. For over thirty years he rented the house from the Atkinson family, but finally he bought it from them.

Peter Tyrer, the licensee of the 'Bull's Head', died in 1855, and he was succeeded by his son, Thomas. Unfortunately the latter died three years later, at the early age of 27. The tenancy was then given to his 75-year-old grandmother, Martha Sutherland.

(ii) Chapel Road
North side
Two terraces of houses were built next to each other in 1849-50 on the north side of Chapel Road on a site now occupied by 'Chapel Court'. The one nearer Cross Street (named 'Lansdowne Terrace') consisted of four terraced houses owned by Thomas Roebuck (*1824-97); the second was owned by Thomas Moore and consisted of five terraced houses. The inhabitants were profes-

sional people (e.g. a tailor, a chain maker, a buyer of haberdashery, a law clerk), and most of them had servants. Thomas Moore also owned a pair of semi-detached houses built at the same time between the terrace and the farm. By the time of the 1851 census, Abraham Hewitt's cottages at 'Cabbage Row' had increased in number to more than thirty; in 1861 there were forty-six. Chapel Lane Farm was sold to Samuel Brooks in 1847. Abraham Hewitt himself retired from the farm in 1848 and took licensed premises near 'Cabbage Row', where he remained for around twenty years. Chapel Lane Farm was now run by John Marsland, who moved there from a farm on Woodhouse Lane, Ashton-on-Mersey. He also owned 11½ acres on Wardle Road, which was all that remained of the Marsland family farm in Rutland Lane. The son of James Marsland (see p.117), John (1796-1877) was born in Sale and lived with his wife, Margaret, five sons, three daughters and two grand-daughters.

South side
The south side remained open fields between the chapel and the cottages facing the canal, but by 1860 the market place had been established behind the cottages which looked on to the canal. These cottages had now been extended to seven in number.

(iii) School Road
North side
In 1842 a large house ('Oak House') was built near William Alderley's house. The owner and occupier was George Kinsey (*1789-1862), a manufacturing chemist born in Knutsford. A pair of large semi-detached houses was built further along in 1850, almost opposite the Township School. This was 'The Grove', the property of William Wilson (*1817-1875), an architect and surveyor born in Barwick (Yorkshire). It was he who was asked to draw up the map of Sale in 1859 which has proved most useful for the writing of this book. He lived in one of the houses and at first the occupant of the other house was Thomas Wheatley, a corn factor and commission agent, also born in Yorkshire (in *1822), but from 1852 to 1873 it was the home of Mrs. Hannah Gallemore, the widow of John Earl Gallemore. She had lived at 'Whitefield House' in Ashton-upon-Mersey, but moved to Sale after her husband's death.

Seven or eight years later two detached houses were built further down, opposite where Hereford Street was built some years later. These were 'Brunswick Villa' (the home of Charles Maguire (1820-63), a shipping merchant born in Dublin) and 'Bridgewater Cottage' (the home of John Scurr Hammond, a corn merchant born in Manchester in *1812).

In 1851 the Congregationalists started to build a new chapel in Montague Road. Their chapel near Sale Bridge was then bought by the Wesleyan Methodists, who realised that their own chapel in Broad Road was becoming too small and was also situated away from the developing centre of Sale. The purchase was made possible by a gift of £400 from John Brogden, of Priory Gate

House. The chapel was re-opened in June 1853 as a Methodist Chapel. This was, however, purely a temporary measure (see below).

Around 1857 four houses were built on a spur off School Road which became 'Partington Place', and a few houses and shops were built between them and the 'Bull's Head'. The residents included Michael McKenna, a tailor who traded there for many years.

James Warren was appointed Assistant Overseer of the Poor and Collector of Highway Rates in 1858; he and his family left the Township School and moved into 'Hawthorn Cottage', which had become vacant by the death of Sarah, the widow of William Alderley, at the end of 1857.

South side
Soon after the opening of the railway several roads were laid out on the south side of School Road. Stanley Grove ran along the line of the modern shopping mall; it was in the shape of a letter 'T', and two terraces, each of four houses, were built along the bar of the 'T', facing School Road. At the time of the 1851 census only two of the houses were inhabited but the others were occupied by the end of the year. One of the earliest residents was William Clegg, whom we shall meet again at a later date (see p.65).

Soon afterwards 'Springfield' was laid out, running parallel to the canal. It took its name from 'Springfield House', the residence of Thomas Atkinson's sister, Maria and her husband. Later it would become 'Springfield Road' and would join up with Sibson Road. A pair of semi-detached houses was built at the corner of Stanley Grove and Springfield. These were named 'Woodville', and the residents in 1861 were Roger Evison (a cotton merchant, born in Manchester in *1810) and Thomas Kelly (a lace manufacturer, born in Dublin in *1812). In the spring of 1861 the Kelly family moved to 'Brooklands House', a new property on Brooklands Road (see p.104).

In 1856 a terrace of three houses was built on the west side of Springfield between Stanley Grove and School Road. The terrace was known as 'Springfield House', and was the home of John Green (a manager), William Keith (a general commission agent) and James Yates (a manufacturer). 'Springfield House' and 'Woodville' for some years were referred to in some directories as 'Stanley Bank'. About the same time two houses were built on the canal side of the road. One was 'Milton Cottage' (1856); for seven years from 1857 this was the home of John Thomas (an auctioneer, born in Manchester in *1804). The other, 'Poplar House' (1857), was for a few years the residence of Alfred Petremont, a pattern designer. From 1861 it was the home of Thomas Marsden, a cotton spinner born in Manchester in *1818. He and his family lived in the house for sixteen years. 'Milton Cottage' was later extended to form two semi-detached houses but was finally demolished to provide an extension to the playground of Springfield School. 'Poplar House' remains; in 1883 St. Paul's Church was built next door, and the house has served as the vicarage since that date. In some documents 'Milton Cottage' and 'Poplar House' are referred to as 'Stanley Place'.

On 25th October 1860, seven years after moving into the temporary premises in the old Independent Chapel, the Wesleyan Methodists opened a large new chapel on a site now occupied by Boots the Chemist. Built by Robert Neill, who also built Aroma Terrace (see p.51), 'Wesley Chapel' was the principal Methodist place of worship in Sale for 103 years until it was finally closed in 1963.

A small number of houses were built at the other end of School Road about the same time. These included two houses on a short spur which later became 'Hayfield Street'.

(iv) Northenden Road
North side

In 1848 a salesman named Josiah Warburton moved into a large house he had built on the canal bank. Born in Bowdon in *1796, he lived with his wife, Elizabeth. He named the house 'Warburton House', and three years later he built a pair of semi-detached houses ('Renshaw Terrace') next to it. The inhabitants of the three houses in 1861 were George Miller, John Lewis and George Alcock. At that time another terrace of four houses was being built; at first known as 'Renshaw Fields' they were later named 'Britannia Grove'. William Chapman's house had been enlarged to a small terrace. One of the inhabitants from 1851 was Richard Ridyard, a coal dealer, born in Little Hulton in *1808. He delivered the coal which came up the canal by boat.

The first houses to be built further down Northenden Road were two houses built in 1849-50, nearly opposite the junction with Derbyshire Road. These were 'Holly Villa' (the home of George Hurlbutt) and 'Laurel Cottage' (the home of John Massey). George Hurlbutt was born in *1799 in Manchester; he became a joiner and glazier with a workshop in St. Mary's Gate. In 1849 he bought a plot of land in Sale on Northenden Road, on which he built his house; he later took a second workshop near the post office on Washway Road. Over the years he became even more prosperous and by 1871 he also owned the small market garden near his house on Northenden Road (formerly James Woodall's farm), a large pair of semi-detached houses named 'Holly Grove' and three of the large houses in Clarendon Road. John Massey (*1797-1863) was a cotton yarn agent with an office at 31, New Cannon Street, Manchester. He was born in Manchester and lived with his wife, Elizabeth, and one servant.

It appears that the 'Temple' had been up-graded by 1851. The residents at that time were Samuel Hinde, a stationer born in Manchester in *1822, and John Earl (born in *1821), a man with a private income. He owned the new buildings on Wharf Road (see p.84). Before moving to the 'Temple', John Earl had lived on Cross Street. He died on the Isle of Man in 1860. The site of the 'Temple' later became the site of the Warwick Cinema, and is now a garage.

As already mentioned, James Woodall's small farm on Northenden Road had become a market garden by 1851. It was bought by George Hurlbutt and from 1855 was run by Joseph Cookson. Soon after 1851 three houses were built between Clarendon Road and Temple Road - two semi-detached houses and one detached; the semis were known as 'Strawberry Bank', while the detached house was 'Strawberry Villa'. The two semis are still lived in, although they now have different names; 'Strawberry Villa', which was actually round round the corner in Beech Road, was demolished some time ago. All three houses were owned by Thomas Lightbourne (1816-1874). Interestingly he did not live in the largest (the detached) house but in one of the semis. He was a wine and spirit dealer, born in Manchester. The other semi was the home of John Hall, a commission agent born in Whitby in *1806. 'Strawberry Villa' was rented by James Pendlebury, cashier to the late Duke of Bridgwater. He was born in Wigan in *1803.

South side
As mentioned above, the Rev. Edward Morris bought a plot of land near the junction of Wardle Road and Northenden Road in 1848, and built a terrace of four houses on it. This was 'Lime Place' and the Rev. Morris himself and his wife, Mary, moved in at the beginning of 1849. Their house was originally number 30 but now it is number 36. Edward Morris was born in Croft Green (Shropshire) in 1816, and had married a girl from Stretford. He was minister of the Sale Independent Chapel for forty years from 1842 and lived in 'Lime Place' until his death in 1889. He retained ownership of three of the houses until he died, but the house at the corner of Wardle Road was sold to its resident (George Greenwood) at an early date.

By 1848 'Beech Cottage' had become the home of Thomas Baxendell (*1792-1874), a 'proprietor of houses' born in Oldham. A row of shops was also built next to it. These later became known as 'Beech Terrace'.

In 1850 a stonemason named John Warriner moved into a house he had built just off Northenden Road. He was born at Whittle-le-Woods (Lancashire) in *1810 and lived with his Salford-born wife, Elizabeth. He died in 1873. The house was named 'Victoria Cottage', and the short street upon which it stood was later named after him. About the same time a joiner named Luke Winstanley moved into Edward Marsland's cottage on Northenden Road. Luke (*1806-1878) was born in Warburton and came to Sale with his wife, Mary. Within a year he had extended the cottage into three cottages and after the Battle of Inkerman (1854, in the Crimean War) the cottages were given the name 'Inkerman Cottages', a name they retain today. One of the residents of the cottages for 27 years from 1851 was George Bloor (1819-1878), a joiner born in Northwich. Later he owned some of the houses on Era Street and Hope Road. Luke Winstanley was very active as a builder in Sale during the 1850's, 1860's and 1870's. One of his buildings was the new Independent chapel in Montague Road (see below). In 1854-5 he built 'Olive Grove', a terrace of four houses near 'Inkerman Cottages'. The inhabitants in 1861 were George Bradbury (a yarn agent, born in Oldham in *1826), Robert B. Lee (an ironsmith born in Middlesex in *1826), Mrs. Elizabeth Woollaston, and Mrs. Elizabeth Shingles (a lodging-house keeper, born in Liverpool in *1816). About the same time, Luke Winstanley established a house and workshop behind 'Olive Grove', in what was to become 'Craven Terrace'. By 1860 he owned 'Inkerman Cottages', 'Olive Grove' and two of the houses on Craven Terrace. He employed 8 joiners, 10 bricklayers and 3 boys. These included his three sons, Matthew, Thomas and William, who were now living in Sale.

The steady increase in population living on the Sale side of the main road meant that the site of St. Martin's Church at the far end of Ashton-on-Mersey was even less convenient than before. Plans were therefore set in motion to build a church in Sale. A plot of land just off Northenden Road was donated by Samuel Brooks, the Manchester banker, and building began. On 14th July, 1854, the new church, St. Anne's, was consecrated and three days later it was opened. The vicar was the Rev. Jonathan J. Cort (see p.46). At first St. Anne's was merely a 'district church', under the wing of St. Martin's, but in 1856 it became an ecclesiastical parish in its own right covering the whole of the township of Sale.

Further building took place at the north end of Northenden Road during the years 1855-9. Craven Terrace was built at right-angles to the road, between Inkerman Cottages and Olive Grove. At first there were three houses ('Oak Terrace') on the north side, facing Luke Winstanley's house and workshop (number 3). During the years 1857-9 the other houses on the east side were built. The last six belonged to Edward Hall, who lived in the end house until after 1876. Born in Settle (Yorkshire) in *1813, he was a master painter. Prior to moving to Craven Terrace he lived for two or three years in one of the 'Inkerman Cottages'.

In 1856-7 a number of houses were built between Wardle Road and the railway station. 'Stamford Terrace' (two pairs of large semi-detached houses) stood next to 'Lime Place'. The inhabitants in 1861 were Arthur Foulkes, James Markland (a cashier, born in Manchester in *1821), John Fullalove (*1821-89, a retired auctioneer, born in Salford) and Frederick Piggott (a silk manufacturer, born in Coventry in *1826). Stamford Place is a short road running between Northenden Road and Montague Road. Two pairs of large semi-detached houses were built on it, facing each other. The inhabitants in 1861 were James Occleston (*1823-1870, a retired silk manufacturer born in Manchester), Isabella Fullalove (*1780-1871, a widow, born in Cartmel, Lancashire), Thomas Turner (commission agent, born in Shropshire in *1811) and William Harrison (a cashier, born in Manchester in *1820). John Fullalove in 'Stamford Terrace' was Isabella's son, and married Jane, the sister of James Occleston. 'Enville Terrace' also consisted of two pairs of semi-detached houses. Only one house was occupied in 1856, but the residents in 1861 were George Rhodes (agent to an oil merchant, born in Tintwistle in *1817), Edward Heslop (stockbroker, born in Yorkshire in *1820), Charles Hope (iron merchant, born in Manchester in *1834) and Elizabeth Lomas (widow). Each of the households in these 'terraces' had either one or two servants. 'Stamford Terrace' and the houses on Stamford Place are still lived in today; 'Enville Terrace' also remains but is now fronted by a single-storey row of shops which was later built in the gardens.

In 1857 'Alma Terrace' was built near the junction with Warrener Street. The houses were later turned into shops. Two years later a hotel was built at the junction of Hope Road and Northenden Road, on the site of James Hope's house. This was the 'Queen's Hotel', managed by Charles Morrison (*1831-65). He was born in Scotland but had come to England and had married a Manchester girl. At the railway station itself lived Richard Wardleworth. Originally a railway porter, he was promoted to be stationmaster at Sale in 1857. Born in Manchester in *1831, he lived with his wife and one servant.

By 1861 William Oldfield's smithy on the corner of Northenden Road and Marsland Road had become a grocer's shop. There were now thirteen other houses and shops between it and Warrener Street.

(v) Clarendon Road

Clarendon Road was a new road laid out in 1850. During the years 1850-1 eight large houses were built along the west side. Those at the north end were at first regarded as being in Broad Road, but by 1853 the name 'Clarendon Road' was established. By the end of March 1851 only one house was occupied - by Edward Robinson, an accountant born in Manchester in *1822. A widower at the age of 29, he lived with his sister-in-law (his house-keeper), his three-year old daughter and one servant. Most of the first occupants of Clarendon Road stayed only a short time; they included Mrs. Elizabeth Frodsham (who ran a girls' boarding school), James McClure (a calico printer), Alfred Midwood (see below), John Greenhough (a builder), and William Butterfield (see p.85). The 1861 census gives us details of the families living in the road in that year. The householders were (from south to north) Johann Geissler (born in Frankfurt), William Skelton, John Whitworth, George Collier, William King, the Rev. Jonathan Cort, John Marsh, and John Moore. Six of these had business premises in Manchester. John Marsh, a pawnbroker and jeweller born in Manchester in *1828, lived in 'Marsholgate House', his house in Clarendon Road, until he died in 1897. John Moore, a manufacturer born in Leicestershire in *1815, lived in Clarendon Road until 1877, while the Rev. Cort was the vicar of the new church (St. Anne's) on Northenden Road. He was born in Yorkshire in *1827. When he and his family came to Sale, they lived in Chapel Road for a few years before moving to Clarendon Road in 1859. Only three of the original houses remain on the west side of Clarendon Road, the rest having been demolished to make way for modern housing (see p.63).

(vi) Temple Road & Oak Road

Thomas Brickell (the licensee of the 'Legh Arms', see p.123) bought a plot of land behind the 'Temple' at the Northenden Road end of Temple Road in

1850. Over the next two years he built a terrace of four houses facing Temple Road on part of the plot. He called them 'Oak Bank'. The inhabitants in 1861 were Thomas Brickell himself, James Gladwin (a dry salter, born in Stockport on *1809), Robert Gore (*1795-1878, a proprietor of houses, born in Runcorn) and William Walker (*1834-1913, a warehouseman, born in Scotland). 'Oak Bank' was followed in 1856-7 by two pairs of semi-detached houses built on the same side of Temple Road. Formerly numbers 25, 27, 43 and 45, they are now numbers 21, 23, 47 and 49. They were owned by Thomas Renshaw, who farmed on Wardle Road. Two years later 'Temple Villa' was built opposite two of Thomas Renshaw's houses in Temple Road; this was a detached house belonging to the resident, Henry Sargeant (*1825-1876). He was a silk finisher born in Bethnal Green (London). Both his first and second wives were called Caroline. 'Temple Villa' was followed in 1860 by two terraces of five and six houses named 'Laurel Bank' and 'Temple Terrace' respectively. 'Laurel Bank' was demolished in the 1950's and a row of modern terraced houses was built on the site at a later date. All the other properties survive.

Oak Road
Two pairs of semi-detached houses were built on Oak Road in 1856. For ten years or so from 1859 the inhabitants of the first pair (now numbers 2 and 4) were George Cuffley (an agent for paper-hanging supplies born in Ipswich *1807) and William Whichello (a warehouseman born in Berkshire in *1808). The second pair (numbers 10 and 12) was built and owned by Thomas Kirtley (*1792-1858) and his son, also named Thomas (b.*1822), builders. One of the inhabitants for nine years from their completion was William Grasby (a commercial traveller born in Lincolnshire in *1828); from 1857 the other house was the home of Miss Emma Faulkner (a lady of private means, born in Manchester in *1833).

(vii) 'Freetown'

Even fifty years after the enclosure of 1806-7 the area which had been 'Sale Moor' was still known by that name. For example, houses on Wardle Road and Northenden Road were listed in directories as being on 'Sale Moor' and the railway station at Sale Bridge was named 'Sale & Sale Moor' from 1856 to 1883. When house-building started on the area which had formerly been the 'Moor', the area was initially known as 'Freetown'. The term included the whole of the area between Hope Road and Derbyshire Road. When the new railway station was opened at Marsland's Bridge in 1859 (see p.28) Samuel Brooks (who had purchased much of the land in the vicinity) insisted that the new railway station be named 'Brooklands'. The new name soon caught on and the term 'Freetown' quickly disappeared. The name 'Sale Moor' is now applied to the area around the 'Legh Arms' at the junction of Northenden Road and Marsland Road, and the term 'Brooklands' refers to the built-up area on each side of Brooklands Road (an area which was farmland in 1859) and part

'Warburton House', on Britannia Grove, was built in 1848 for Josiah Warburton (see p.43).

of Marsland Road.

Three new roads were laid out around 1852-3. These were originally 'North Street', 'South Street' and 'West Street', but in 1867 their names were changed to the more genteel-sounding 'Poplar Grove', 'South Grove' and 'West Grove'. For ten years or so Poplar Grove and South Grove did not run right through to Hope Road as they do now, but stopped short in the fields between West Grove and Hope Road. House-building started in 1851, and progress was as follows:-

Poplar Grove
Moss Cottage (no.4) was completed by the end of 1855. It was the home of Willam Later, and after his death, his widow, Ellen, continued to live there for ten years. 1856 saw the building of 'Percival Terrace' and 'Northwood Cottage' (no.46). 'Percival Terrace' was owned by Mrs. Phoebe Cartwright, who lived in one of the houses for over twenty-five years. Two other residents of 'Percival Terrace' remained there for over twenty years. They were Mrs. Mary Anderson (a widow born in Wrenbury in *1814) and John Dutton (a fundholder, born in Westmorland in *1819). One of the early residents of 'Northwood Cottage' was Richard de Lannoy (1794-1880), a silk broker born in Surrey. In 1860 three identical pairs of semi-detached houses were completed on the opposite side of the road. These were 'Beech Villa' (originally nos.11-13, now nos.11A-15A), 'Lime Villa', and 'Brooklyn Villa' (the last-mentioned took its name from one of its first residents - Walter Brook). One of the long-staying residents of 'Lime Villa' was John Nodal, a cashier to a tea merchant, who lived there for over twenty years. 'South Villas' (two semi-detached houses) were added in 1861. They had a number of residents over the years. They are now nos. 40-42.

South Grove
'Marchfield Terrace' and 'Summer Villa' were built by the end of 1855. They were followed by 'South View' in 1857 and the five cottages in 1858. Mrs Betty Derbyshire lived in no.28 (in 'South View') for over twenty years. She was a 'proprietor of houses', born in Chorlton (Manchester) in *1804. Captain John Wight built a house in South Grove in 1859. This was no.20; it never had a name. Captain Wight was a 'pensioner' (presumably from the army or the navy) born in Scotland in *1803. He lived in South Grove until his death in 1882. Thomas Johnson built 'Johnson's Villa' in 1860. Now numbers 30-34, it seems that at first it was one house, and then was extended in stages. Thomas Johnson (*1802-81) seems to have built a number of houses in Sale and then sold them almost immediately, moving with his family elsewhere. He was a retired publican, born in Failsworth (Manchester).

West Grove
The first house to be built was 'Rose Villa', built in 1852-3 by Dr. Peter Royle,

Two of the houses of 'Aroma Terrace', Wardle Road. They were built around 1853 (see p.51).

who lived in the neighbouring 'Vernon Lodge'. The tenant for some years was John S. Wilson, a salesman born in Manchester in *1823. 'Holly Cottage' (number 5) was completed by the end of 1855, and 'Park Cottage' and 'Ivy Cottage' followed four years later. These three houses had a series of residents over the years.

(viii) Wardle Road

Even though Wardle Road was situated near to the railway, for over ten years it experienced little change. The 1851 census shows just one house under construction between Ann Marsland's house and Peter Wardle's farm. This was probably 'Moss Grove House', a pair of semi-detached houses on the corner of Poplar Grove. It was owned by William Bridge (1808-1896), a retired cloth agent, born in Manchester. He let the house to several tenants, including his son William, before he himself moved into it in the 1860's. Around 1853 four houses were built near the Northenden Road end of Wardle Road by the Salford builder, Robert Neill (who later built the foundations of Manchester's Central Station). The houses were named 'Aroma Terrace' and later became numbers 4, 6, and 8 in Wardle Road plus 'Brookfield House' (the last named was set back from Wardle Road and later became number 19, Montague Road). The original occupants were George Ollivant, Mrs. Ann Blackburn, Mrs. Mary Emmett and John Allen. George Ollivant (*1804-76) was a 'foreign merchant' with an office in Lever Street, Manchester. He was born in Salford and lived with his wife, Mildred, three sons, two daughters and one servant. Mrs. Blackburn ran a boarding school. John Allen was a 'warehouseman'; he was born in Leicestershire in *1803 and lived in 'Brookfield House' with his wife, Mary, four daughters and two sons. His position as 'warehouseman' must have been different from the modern understanding of the term, as he and his wife had three servants. Within three or four years number 8 had its own name - 'Heathfield House'. Two of the houses are still there (with different names), but 'Heathfield' and 'Brookfield House' were demolished to make way for modern semi-detached housing.

Ann Marsland died in 1853 at the age of 80. Two years previously she had sold her house to John Shockledge (born in Newcastle-under-Lyne in *1794). He was a grocer and tea dealer and the house became a shop. In 1856 John Kershaw Clough bought a plot of land next to Wardle's Farm Here he built a house which he called 'Ebenezer House'. He was a smallware dealer with premises in Radnor Street, Hulme. In addition he was a local preacher in the Wesleyan Methodist Circuit. He was born in Bolton in *1802 and died in 1881. Peter Wardle died in 1854, and he was succeeded by Thomas Renshaw from Whitehall Farm. As the land was gradually sold off for house-building Wardle's Farm ceased to be a farm and became a market garden.

Two further pairs of semi-detached houses were built on Wardle Road. One, built in 1854-5, was 'Northern View' (present numbers 54-56), the home of Jabez Stafford and James R. Walker. The other, built five years later on the corner of Poplar Grove, was the home of William Thornber and John Aked. These are now numbers 46-48. William Thornber (*1830-84) was an export merchant born in Tottington near Bury. Later he moved to 'Wardle House' (see p.66). All four houses are still lived in today.

(ix) Montague Road

As mentioned above, in 1851 the Congregationalists sold their chapel near Sale Bridge to the Wesleyan Methodists. A new chapel was built by Luke Winstanley opposite the end of Stamford Place. The total cost was £2200, and the land was given by Samuel Brooks. The new chapel was opened on 18th May, 1852, and the new road was named 'Montague Road'. The first houses were built along it soon afterwards. Three pairs of semi-detached houses were built at the Hope Road end in 1856; these were named 'Brighton Place' and were owned by the Misses Hewitt, who lived in Chapel Road. One of the residents was Mrs. Mary Ann Bundock, who ran a school for young ladies. In the following year two other pairs of semi-detached houses were built next to them; one pair was named 'Victoria Place', and the other pair consisted of 'Albion Villa' and 'Derby House'. These were some of the very few houses built by Samuel Brooks in Sale. ('Derby House' later became number 6, Stamford Place). The inhabitants of Montague Road in 1861 were all professional people (merchants, attorneys, school-teachers, etc.) with servants. One of the first residents of 'Victoria Place' was William Foyster, Samuel Brooks's solicitor. He was born in Lincoln in *1816 and his firm, Hulme, Foyster & Foyster, had premises at 22, Brazennose Street, Manchester. The six houses belonging to the Misses Hewitt survive today, although in a much-altered state; Samuel Brooks's houses have been demolished.

(x) Derbyshire Road

In 1848 Joseph Moore built two cottages near the junction of Derbyshire Road and Marsland Road. One of these was the home of John Gough (*1822-87), an agricultural labourer who later took over Brogden's Farm. The other had several residents until 1856, when John Howitt and his family moved in. John (*1808-83) was a joiner, brought to Sale from Nottinghamshire by John Morley (see below). Prior to living on Derbyshire Road, he and his family lived on Cross Street.

In 1850 a builder named John Morley (1809-1882) moved into Sale; born in Ratcliffe (Nottinghamshire), he lived with his wife, Sarah, in a house at Moor Nook rented from John Brogden of Priory Gate House. He bought a plot of land on the south side of Derbyshire Road and built three large houses on it, naming the small estate 'Holly Bank'. One house was detached, and the other two were pairs of semi-detached houses. In 1851 the first inhabitants moved in; they were John Richardson (a clerk in an export warehouse, born in *1810), George Brewer (an oil merchant, born in *1823), Henry Stevenson (1811-1876, a landed proprietor) and John Cross (a cotton agent, born in

*1806). They were soon joined by William King, a merchant born in *1810. Each of these households had one or two servants. In 1856 John Morley himself moved into a new house ('Windsor Cottage') he had built at the end of the short cul-de-sac. The houses of 'Holly Bank' still survive, but the site of 'Windsor Cottage' is now part of the Grammar School playing fields. By 1861 John Morley was describing himself as a 'landed proprietor', and for fifteen years or so Derbyshire Road was known as 'Morley's Lane'.

John Morley built a fourth house in 'Holly Bank' in 1861. This was larger than the houses built ten years previously, and the new house was bought by one of the residents of the existing houses. He was Alfred Watkin (*1825-1875), a merchant, JP and alderman, born in Salford.

(xi) Washway Road

N.B. see the note at the beginning of the section on Cross Street (p.40).

A terrace of 7 houses was built in 1851 between New Chester and Sale Terrace. The new terrace was named 'Elm Terrace', and the inhabitants in 1851 were professional people - a schoolmaster, a general agent, a pawnbroker, a clerk to the Highways Department and an annuitant. A beerhouse was also built between 'New Chester' and the new terrace; later this became the 'Vine Inn'. From 1853 to 1866 licensee was John Jackson, who was born at Cartmel in *1814.

Six years later a row of eight shops was built near the junction of School Road and Washway Road. Among the shopkeepers and tradesmen who rented these premises were George Hurlbutt and George Birkenhead. The former was a successful glazier and plumber from Manchester (see p.43). George Birkenhead (*1809-1875) was born at Marston (near Northwich). He was originally a shoemaker, living with his wife, Eliza, in premises next to the 'Wagon & Horses' on Cross Street. Next door was a shop belonging to Samuel Brindley, a tailor and draper, born in Derbyshire. Samuel (*1826-90) was appointed Sale's first postmaster in 1858. In 1864 he moved into a new shop in School Road and George Birkenhead took over his premises and also his job as postmaster. A large detached house ('West Bank') was built in 1859 on the corner of Washway Road and a short spur which later became Sibson Road. The original owner moved out in 1861, and the house became the home of Joseph Kay, a commission agent born in Salford in *1825. He and his family lived there for over thirty years. A pair of semi-detached houses was built in 1860 on the opposite corner of the short spur. These were called 'Leamington Villas' (later numbered 35-37). Here lived William Sanderson, a leather factor born in Sheffield in *1828 and Thomas Hamilton, a bachelor 'gentleman', born in Manchester in *1806.

Samuel Roebuck of 'Sale Bank' bought most of the land between the modern Sibson Road and Roebuck Lane. He had John Royle's old house rebuilt and extended to become 'Mayfield Cottage' (later, just 'Mayfield'). This was rented from 1852 for nine years by Llewelyn Hanmer, a cotton yarn agent, born in the Channel Islands in *1820. He and his wife, Martha, had 11 children and 1 servant. Samuel Roebuck also built a very large house between 'Mayfield Cottage' and 'Sale Bank' in 1851. Named 'Broadoaks', it stood 150 yards from the main road in extensive grounds (the exact position of the house was at the end of the modern Wickenby Drive). It was in fact divided into two houses, and the original tenants were John Pilling and Richard Zahn. We have no information about John Pilling as he moved away within a few years. His half of 'Broadoaks' was then rented by Alfred Midwood of Grundy, Midwood & Co. (merchants). Alfred Midwood was born in Manchester in *1823. He and his wife Grace moved with their three servants to 'Broadoaks' from Clarendon Road, where they had been living. Richard Zahn (*1823-1875) was a South American merchant with premises at 35, Dickinson Street, Manchester. He was born in Prussia and his wife, Anne, was born in Nottinghamshire. They had four servants. The house was demolished around 1920 and the gardens became an estate of semi-detached houses on a road named appropriately enough 'Broadoaks Road'. Samuel Roebuck also built a small house in the grounds of 'Sale Bank' in 1860. This was 'Sale Bank Cottage', although it was later known as 'Ivy Cottage'. The first tenant was David Gow, a merchant born in Scotland in *1823. The house survives today as the last vestige of Samuel Roebuck's estate, but, having been unoccupied for many years, it is in a very delapidated state.

Dr. Henry Ollier was awarded the Royal Humane Society's Medal in 1844. Two young girls had fallen into the River Mersey, and he was instrumental in reviving them. There is no record of what William Brownhill (the man who actually went into the water and rescued them) received. Dr. Ollier died in 1852, and his widow, Ellen (*1809-1881), continued to live in 'Roseville Cottage' until 1861, when she moved into Poplar Grove.

By 1856 four cottages had been built next to William Royle's cottage on Roebuck Lane. The five cottages were named 'Renshaw Cottages' (after their owner, William Renshaw) and in 1861 the inhabitants were John Twiss (timber merchant), Willam Royle, Joseph Kelsall (gardener), Thomas Jackson (coachman) and John Whitelegg (labourer).

1861-1876

(i) Cross Street

It seems that the 'Bull's Head' was run by Martha Sutherland until 1864, when she died at the age of 80. Samuel Whittle then took over. He was followed four years later by William Robinson, who was born in Ashley in *1831. He stayed at the 'Bull's Head' for ten years. The Joynson family continued to live at 'Ashfield'. When Sale became a Local Government District in 1867 William Joynson became the Chairman of the new District Board. A series of new streets was built between the 'Bull's Head' and 'Ashfield' in 1869-70. These were Mason Street (nine terraced houses), Wilson Street (fifteen houses) and Eliza Street. The last-named contained only three houses and the Union Club. The origin of the street names is unclear, apart from Wilson Street, which was named after the owner of the houses, Joseph Wilson, a shirt manufacturer. The gap between Wilson Street and Eliza Street was filled in the following two years by the building of Eden Place (6 houses) and several shops. The latter included a shoemaker and a tailor. By 1876, however, there were still only two buildings between Eliza Street and Chapel Road.

(ii) Chapel Road

Existing properties

During the years 1865-6 the two semi-detached houses near Chapel Road Farm were converted into one large detached house. This was named 'Brook House' after its owner and resident, William Brooks, a brewer and spirit merchant, born in Manchester in *1827. Abraham Hewitt ran his beer-shop until 1869 and John Marsland remained at the farm until his death in 1877.

New buildings - north side

Various new properties were built on Chapel Road during the period 1861-1876. On the north side four houses were built between Cross Street and 'Lansdowne Terrace'. These were the homes of George Wright (coachman), Mary Ingram, Robert Birchall (watchmaker) and Henry Russell (upholsterer). One of the largest developments in Sale began in 1869, when Egerton Street was laid out. It was approached from Chapel Road via a short street named 'Bridgewater Street'. By 1871 it contained fifty houses, and finally there were eighty-six. The houses on the east side of Egerton Street backed on to the canal, and at first the street was named 'Canal Street'. All the houses were owned by John Rhodes, who lived on Washway Road.

New buildings - south side

On the south side a Drill Hall was built behind the old Independent Chapel, which was now the 'Sale Institute'. Next to the Drill Hall were the Police station and the Market Place. Round the latter about twenty cottages were built over the years 1862-66, all belonging to Abraham Hewitt (who also owned all the cottages of 'Cabbage Row' on the opposite side of the road). One of the houses, 35, Chapel Road, was a beershop, and Arthur Twigge sold ale here for over twenty years from 1867; he was born in Derbyshire in *1844. The 1871 census shows that two police officers lived in the houses round the Market Place. The Drill Hall survives as part of a Youth Club.

In 1869 a pair of semi-detached houses were built at the end of a new street running off Chapel Road. One of them was the home of George Ashcroft (*1833-1918), a slater born in Ashton-on-Mersey. He was possibly the nephew of the George Ashcroft who lived on Cross Street, and who probably owned the houses. A further eight houses were built next to them by Thomas Lamb (a plumber who lived in School Road). They were joined in the following year by eight other houses on the opposite (west) side of the street. These were owned by William Joynson, on whose land they were built. The street was then named 'Joynson Street'. Also in 1870 a terrace of seven houses was built facing 'Lansdowne Terrace'. These were 75-87 Chapel Road.

(iii) School Road

Existing properties

When George Kinsey died in 1862, his widow, Sarah, continued to live in 'Oak House' until she herself died in 1874. James Warren and his family still lived in 'Hawthorn Cottage'. When the Sale Urban District was set up in 1867, the District Council Offices were established in part of James Warren's house. After Mrs. Kinsey's death, the Local Board purchased 'Oaklands' (as Oak House' was now called) at a cost of £1300, and the Warren family moved to 'Alma Terrace' on Northenden Road.

The Wilsons moved from 'The Grove' to a new house ('Harper Hill') built on Derbyshire Road in 1862. 'The Grove' was then bought by George V. Ryder (1803-1888), an insurance manager born in Cheshire. Mrs. Gallemore continued to live in the other half of the house until her death in Knaresborough in 1873. 'Oak Cottage' (the Leeds house) had a succession of owners between 1861 and 1876. One of them was Edwin Heaps, who built Edwin and Ada Terraces on Essex (later 'Norris') Road. He was a cabinet maker born in Macclesfield in *1834. The name 'Oak Cottage' was changed to 'The Poplars', and the house was demolished when this part of School Road was developed in the 1890's. 'Bridgewater Cottage' and 'Brunswick Villa' also had various owners. The latter also had a change of name - to 'Gorse Cottage'. From 1870 the tenant of 'Bridgewater Cottage' was Leonard Hunt, a paint merchant born in Richmond (Yorkshire) in *1832.

Several of the residents in Springfield and Stanley Grove stayed for more than fifteen years. They included John S. Wilson in 'Springfield House', Elizabeth Horrocks in 'Milton Cottage', and Elizabeth Croom and Elizabeth Brophy in Stanley Grove.

New buildings - north side
Very few new buildings were built on the north side of School Road between 1861 and 1876. Orchard Place, a short cul-de-sac of eight houses, was built in 1864. It took its name from the orchard which was formerly on the site. A number of new shops were also built near the 'Bull's Head', and four shops and houses between 'Gorse Cottage' and 'The Poplars', but in 1876 three quarters of the north side of School Road still consisted of green fields or gardens.

New buildings - south side
In 1861 the south side of School Road was as it had been sixteen years earlier - a row of four houses at the Washway Road end, the Township School further up, and the rest fields. The only new building on School Road itself was the Wesleyan Chapel (the houses on Stanley Grove and Springfield were set back from School Road). By 1871, however, the south side of School Road was continuously built up from Washway Road to the canal. Most of the buildings were now shops, with the obvious exceptions of the Township School and the Wesleyan Chapel. The new buildings included 'Heywood Bank', which consisted of ten houses and shops belonging to the Richardson family. These included the first Co-op premises in Sale (1869 - the CWS had been formed only seven years previously) and the first bank in Sale - Parr's Bank, which took over a shop on the corner of Hereford Street in 1873. Two of the shops on the south side of School Road which became well-known were that of J.W. Clough (draper, near the corner of Stanley Grove) and of that Henry Wovenden (chemist, near the station). John W. Clough was one of the sons of J.K. Clough of 'Ebenezer House' on Wardle Road. He died in 1878 at the age of 27, and his mother then looked after the business. Three other shops of interest were those of Mrs. Maria Crompton (who in 1861 sold boots and shoes and in 1871 sold books and toys, and also ran a servants' registry), Francis Robinson (who made and sold 'celebrated Cheshire sausages and polonies') and Thomas Lamb (*1837-81, a plumber who owned half of Joynson Street and many of the large houses on Wardle Road).

A pair of semi-detached houses was built on the north side of Stanley Grove in 1872. The Township School was enlarged in 1854, in 1861 and again in 1876, when an infants' department was built next door on the corner of Springfield Road.

(iv) Sibson Road
North side
At first Sibson Road was a short stub, running from Washway Road. This led to a pair of semi-detached houses built in 1867. At the time the houses were described as being on Washway Road. They belonged to the executors of Joseph Sandbach, whose widow lived in 'Yew Villas' on Washway Road. Her son, William, was one of the residents from 1869. He was a manufacturer born in Manchester in *1845. In 1868 the road was extended to meet Springfield Road

at right angles.

Three pairs of semi-detached houses, 'York Terrace', were built in 1870. They were owned by one of the residents, Charles Denton, a joiner born in Pontefract in *1819. The site is now a grassy space in front of the multi-storey car-park. As they were being built, two detached houses were nearing completion between them and Hereford Street. These were the homes of John Wonstall (a salesman born in Liverpool in *1825) and the Rev. Thomas Gibson (a schoolteacher born in Ireland in *1837). Three detached houses were built in 1871-2 between the Sandbach house and the corner of Hereford Street. These were the homes of Robert Stracey (a warehouse manager born in Liverpool in *1842), William Rae (a merchant born in Scotland in *1840) and William Nickson (a merchant born in Stafford in *1834).

South side

The Atkinson family (see p.31) owned the land on the south side of Sibson Road. 'Sibson' was the maiden name of Elizabeth, the wife of Joseph Atkinson (1828-1901). In 1869 Joseph, the oldest surviving son of Thomas Atkinson, built a large house ('The Laurels') in an acre of ground on the south side of the road. When he and his family moved to Ashton-on-Mersey two years later, 'The Laurels' became the home of his unmarried sister, Jane (1829-1911), who was a member of the Manchester Society of Woman Painters. About the same time another large house was completed next to it; this house also had an acre of garden. Named 'Moorside', it was situated opposite the end of Hereford Street and was the home of George Rooke (1828-1911), a manufacturing chemist born in Manchester. He had married Elizabeth, the sister of Joseph and Jane Atkinson. The grounds of the house stretched to the back of 'Broadoaks'. Part of the site is now occupied by a block of flats appropriately named 'Moorside Court'.

Friars Road took its name from 'The Friars', the name of the house in which Jane, the wife of Thomas Atkinson, had lived before her marriage. In 1870 a retired grocer named Joseph Handley built a terrace of four houses ('Handley Terrace') on the west side of Friars Road. Born in Sedbergh in *1809, he lived in one of the houses. The only other building was a girls' school on the other side of the road and run by the Rev. Gibson and his wife, Jane.

(v) Hereford Street

Hereford Street runs from School Road to Sibson Road. It was so-called because 'The Friars' (see above) was in Hereford. It is difficult today to visualise Hereford Street as it was in 1876. Then it was a street of smart town houses; now there are no houses at all - the road has a supermarket on one side and the shops of Market Walk on the other.

The houses were built between 1865 and 1870, starting at the School Road end. Among the first houses to be built were the two houses and workshop belonging to James and William Smith, builders from Derbyshire. They built a number of houses in Sale, including some on Hope Road. There were five detached houses on the site of the supermarket (between John Street and Sibson Road). Four of these belonged to Samuel Brindley, who had a draper's shop on School Road. The fifth, 'Midmoor Cottage' on the corner of John Street, was the home for many years of William Wilkinson, a 'shipman' born in Yorkshire in *1833.

There was a small square halfway along the east side of Hereford Street. On the north side of this square was a terrace of four houses called 'Lily Bank'. Most of the houses on the east side of Hereford Street had names. Number 1 was set back from the street itself, almost behind number 3. Built in 1867, it was called 'Hereford House', and the resident from 1871 was Charles Russell, a timber merchant. The road on the east and south sides of the square was named 'Elizabeth Street', taking its name from the wife of Joseph Atkinson. The name 'Elizabeth Street' appears in the rate books for the 1860's, but does not figure in street directories until sixty years later. The large house on the corner of Elizabeth Street and Hereford Street was 'Vanner House', the home of Walter Nicholson, an umbrella manufacturer born in Liverpool in *1839. Next door was 'Rock Villa', the home of Richard Pearn, a tailor born in *1838 in Dawlish (Devon). His house was completed in 1870.

John Street ran from Hayfield Street to Hereford Street. On the north side there were eight houses (six built in 1874 by James Smith of Hereford Street) and on the south side there were three ('Prospect House' built by Thomas Johnson in 1874 and two owned by Samuel Brindley, dating from 1876)

(vi) Northenden Road to the 'Legh Arms'
Existing properties
There were several changes of ownership and tenancy during the years 1861-1876, especially in the houses nearer the railway station ('Lime Place', Stamford Place, 'Stamford Terrace' and 'Enville Terrace'). There were other changes in 'Laurel Cottage' and 'Holly Villa'. John Massey of 'Laurel Cottage' died in 1863 and the house was then bought by William Hamer, an auctioneer born in Lancaster in *1815. He lived in the house until his death in 1875-6. George Hurlbutt in 'Holly Villa' died in 1874. 'Laurel Cottage' is now the 'Hazelmere Hotel', but 'Holly Villa' has been replaced by two modern houses,. one of them appropriately named 'Holly Villa'. The small farm formerly belonging to Robert Barlow was now run by William Williamson, who was born in Ashton-on-Mersey in *1807. 'Victoria Cottage' (John Warriner's house) had a series of tenants after 1864. These included Douglas Noble (see p.89) and William Rylance (see p.90).

In 1866 the parish of St. Anne's became a 'civil parish' in addition to being an 'ecclesiastical parish'. It was now recognised as a separate parish for local government purposes.

'Strawberry Bank', on Northenden Road was built for Thomas Lightbourne (see p.44).

New properties - north side
In 1861 George Hurlbutt built a pair of large semi-detached houses, which he named 'Holly Grove'. They were approached from the road by a 100-yard-long drive. One of the residents for over twelve years from 1865 was Dixon Losh, another of the Losh brothers (see p.85). His income was derived from railway stocks; he was born in Carlisle in *1809. The houses have gone but the drive remains. Another resident was Leonard Edminson, who later moved to Clarendon Road.

By 1862 the houses on 'Renshaw Fields' (Britannia Grove) had increased to eight. One of the residents was Thomas Howard, a platelayer on the railway, who was unfortunately killed at Bowdon station in 1863. In the same year (1863) a retired farmer bought a plot of land on Northenden Road between 'Holly Villa' and 'Holly Grove'. Here he built a house which he called 'Lee House'. Elias Roberts (*1811-1873) was born in Denbighshire. Since his death his house has had several names, the current name being 'Park House'. In the following year 'Apna Villa' was built between Beech Road and Oak Road. The first owner was Isaac Mason, but for nine years from 1868 it was the home of Samuel Deacon (*1823-1900), a cotton yarn agent born in Manchester. 1871 saw the completion of the first shops near the junction with Broad Road. These consisted of three shops situated nearly opposite Enville Terrace. These were a plumber's, confectioner's, and a lock-up shop. The plumber, Robert Collier, owned all three houses. One of them is now an Indian restaurant. The row of shops was later extended to the junction with Broad Road. Another two shops were built at the other end of Northenden Road, in front of the old Barlow Farm.

1870 saw the beginning of a period in which many large houses were built along Northenden Road. The first houses on the north side of the road were a pair of very large semi-detached houses on the corner of Irlam Road and Northenden Road. One house ('Claremont') was in Irlam Road and the other ('Southfield House') was in Northenden Road. The houses were empty for a time, but in the following year 'Southfield House' became the home of Mrs. Olive Aspinall. At the same time another large house was completed on the opposite corner of Irlam Road. This was 'Ferrol Lodge'; it had several owners in the short period 1872-6. 1873 saw the building of a large pair of semi-detached houses next to 'Southfield House'. One, 'Ventnor Villa', was the home of William Wadsworth (*1829-89), a smallware manufacturer born in Manchester. The other, 'Roundthorn', was the home of Mrs. Elizabeth Dunn, a widow. 'Ventnor Villa' is now named 'Glan-navan'. In the following year another pair of large semi-detached houses were completed almost next door; these were 'Briarleigh' and 'Oak Villa'. 'Briarleigh' was the home of Henry Thorpe, a manufacturer born in Macclesfield in *1832, while 'Oak Villa' was the home of William Henry Boddington. 'Oak Villa' has been demolished and 'Briarleigh' has been drastically rebuilt. The short road upon which 'Roundthorn' and 'Briarleigh' had their entrances later became 'Cheltenham

Drive'.

The Presbyterians opened a new church on 16th February, 1874. Situated opposite 'Stamford Terrace', it had a tall spire which made it a well-known landmark in the centre of Sale. It was closed and demolished in 1968. An office-block now stands on the site. Lastly, in 1876 Alice Street (which ran off Temple Road) and Wilkinson Street were laid out and the first few houses occupied.

New properties - south side

In 1863 Edward Hall built two detached houses on the west side of Craven Terrace. At first numbered 8 and 10, they later became 14 and 16. Around the same time, a school was built behind St. Anne's Church. The headmaster for over thirty-six years was Edward Yates (1834-1915). He was born in Pattingham, Staffordshire. Four years later (1867) Luke Winstanley built four houses facing John Warriner's house ('Victoria Cottage'). The houses were named 'Olive Mount'; the street was given the name of 'Warrener Street' (wrongly spelt with an 'e'). In the same year Luke Winstanley also built a terrace of four houses on Northenden Road, naming it 'North Bank'. The first inhabitants were Alfred Knowles (a commission agent), John Sampson (a commercial traveller), David Walker (also a commercial traveller) and Samuel Titmas (a railway advertising agent).

A number of large houses were built between Derbyshire Road and St. Anne's Church in the years 1871 to 1875. In order from north to south, these were 'Rosslyn' (completed in 1873), 'Summerlea' (1872), 'Heathville' (1873), 'Thorncliffe' (1873), 'Huntley House' (1871). Two more, 'Kent Villa' (1874), and 'Brookfield' (1875), were completed between St. Anne's and Trinity Chapel. All were detached with the exception of 'Rosslyn', which was one of a pair of semi-detached houses, the other being round the corner in Derbyshire Road. Alfred Mitchell and his family lived in 'Rosslyn'; he was a master tailor born in Manchester in *1846.'Summerlea' was from 1875 the home of Alexander Fraser, a merchant born in Edinburgh in *1824; 'Heathville' was the home of a widow, Mrs. Jessie Waddell, who was born in Dumfries in *1812. 'Summerlea' and 'Heathville' were later joined together and now form the 'Dane Lodge Hotel'. 'Thorncliffe' was the home of James Smith, a retired merchant born in Ashby-de-la-Zouch in *1816; 'Huntley House' had several owners in the period 1871-1876; it is now a children's nursery. 'Kent Villa' was the home of William Pollitt, a railway officer born in Ashton-under-Lyne in *1842, and 'Brookfield' was the home of John Keal, who moved there from Beaufort Road. In 1876 three other large houses were nearing completion on the south side of Northenden Road; two of these ('Vermont' and 'Elsinore') were owned by John Keal.

The Wesleyan Methodists saw that a new chapel was needed near the rapidly-developing area round Temple Road and Derbyshire Road. On 30th September 1875 they therefore opened a new church on Northenden Road. This was Trinity Chapel, and the small chapel on Broad Road was then closed. Trinity Chapel itself was closed in 1980, although worship still continues in the converted schoolroom behind the church. The latter then became a series of offices.

(vii) Clarendon Road

The houses on the west side of the road remained without any additions. The numbering of the houses had several gaps where plots were still vacant. Some of the new residents in the 1860's were John Richardson, a solicitor born in Northampton in *1833, Andrew Hamilton, an accountant born in Salford in *1841 (he owned a number of houses in Sale, including 'Ferrol Lodge'), Henry Acton, a newspaper editor, born in Exeter in *1828, and Robert B. Lee, who had previously lived in 'Olive Grove' (see p.44). He owned a number of houses in Sale (including 'Claremont' and 'Southfield House').

Four new large houses were built on the east side of the road. James Roby lived at 'Clarendon House' (number 4, built in 1862), Leonard Edminson lived next door at 'Glendale House' (built in 1867), Alfred Rogers lived at number 8 (built in 1867) and the Rev Jonathan Cort moved across the road into number 10 in 1868. He and his family lived there until his death in 1884. Alfred Rogers was a dentist, born in London in *1829; he lived in 'Holly Bank' before moving to Clarendon Road. Leonard Edminson was a foreign merchant, born in Northumberland in *1830 and James Roby was a merchant, born in Tamworth in *1823. All the households in Clarendon Road had two or three servants. The Acton and Edminson families remained in Clarendon Road for over twenty years.

Five of these houses are still lived in today. These were nos. 5, 15 and 25 (now numbered 15, 53 and 71), and nos. 8 and 10 ('The Vicarage'). The last two are now named 'Brackenhoe' and 'Holly Lodge'.

(viii) Temple Road & Oak Road

Between 1861 and 1876 a number of new houses were built on the vacant plots on Temple Road. Two terraces of three houses were built in 1864 on the north-west side, opposite 'Temple Villa'. They were built by two brothers, who each owned and lived in one terrace. James and John Heywood were market gardeners, born in Timperley in *1825 and *1829 respectively. In 1871 a large house was completed at the corner of Temple Road and Broad Road, opposite 'Claydon House'. This was 'Syrian Villa', the home of Abdullah Trad and his family. He was a shipper of cotton goods, born in Syria in *1838. He had married a girl from Bradford and had become a British subject. While their house was being built, the Trads lived in one of the new houses on the south-east side of Temple Road. Two of these were built in 1866, three in 1869, and a further two in 1870. The gap between these houses and Northenden Road was finally closed when a further three houses were built in 1871. All the houses existing in 1876 are still there today, except for 'Laurel

Bank', which was demolished in the 1950's. 'Syrian Villa' is now 'Sylvan Villa', and the entrance has been moved on to Broad Road.

Oak Road
The Whichello family lived in number 4 until 1873, when they moved to John Street. The Cuffley family remained in no.2. Both the Grasby family and Miss Faulkner left their houses in 1867 and the houses had a number of tenants after this date. Two new houses were built in 1864. Each consisted of a pair of semi-detached houses; they later became numbers 1 and 3 and numbers 6 and 8. William Irwin, a printer born in Wigton (Cumbria), lived in no.1 for over twelve years. Number 6 and 8 were built by Thomas Brickell on the plot he had purchased. In 1867 two further houses were built on Oak Road. These were detached, the homes of James Alcock (no.14) and John Unsworth (no.7). The latter (*1810-95) was a retired engineer born in Leigh (Lancashire). In 1871 he extended his house to form two semi-detached houses. Lastly, in 1875 two more houses (9 and 11) were built. These were also owned by John Unsworth.

(ix) Hope Road
When Charles Morrison, the licensee of the 'Queen's Hotel' died in 1865 at the early age of 34, his widow Edith took over for several years. In 1869 she installed a manager - John Parker, who was born in Derbyshire in *1835. The first houses built on Hope Road backed on the railway station. These were five pairs of semi-detached houses (nos. 4-22), which were built in the years 1862-4. The appearance of most of these houses has been much impaired by 'modernisation'.

Building began on the opposite side of the road in 1864. The first house was the large detached house at the junction with Northenden Road - 'Sale Bridge House'. It was the home of Herbert Renshaw, a member of the Renshaw family of doctors. He was born in Manchester in 1835 and died in 1922. About the same time, a terrace of four cottages was built further down Hope Road, at right angles to the road. These were always referred to as the 'Model Cottages', and later became part of Thorn Grove, although they were never allocated any house numbers. On 5th August, 1866 the Roman Catholics opened their first chapel in Sale (St. Joseph's) near the junction of Hope Road and Montague Road. The building became a school in 1885 when a new and larger church was built nearer to Montague Road. About the same time (1867) a terrace of three houses was built next to the chapel; they were named 'Alma Terrace' and for a number of years one of the houses was the home of the priest, Father Michael Crawley, who served the Sale church for nearly forty years. 1868 saw the building of eleven houses to the south of the Catholic Chapel. The last of these ('Rose Bank', formerly no. 59, now no.77) stood by itself, 150 yards from the others. For forty years it was the home of Henry Baguley, junior, a coppersmith. He was born in Birmingham in *1840. His father was also a coppersmith with premises near Sale station.

'Thorn Grove House' and the terrace of six houses joined to it were built in 1868. These were followed in the following year by a terrace of eight houses at right angles to the first terrace. The end house of the second terrace ('Beech House') was larger than the others, and this was the home of Thomas Sanders, who owned both terraces of houses. He was a blacksmith born in Manchester in *1831. The two terraces and the four model cottages made up three sides of a square (the side nearest to Hope Road was open until a later date). Another street was built in 1869 further down Hope Road; this was Era Street. Originally six pairs of semis, the houses were added to and modified at a later date. They are still lived in today.

In 1872 building began to the south of 'Rose Bank'. William Smith of Hereford Street built a pair of semi-detached houses ('Hope Bank') between Poplar Grove and South Grove. Two years later he added an identical pair of houses next to them. At the same time (1874) his brother James built another pair of semi-detached houses on Hope Road. These were 'Ellesmere House' (now no.79) and 'Salisbury House' (now no.81). All these houses had a number of residents over the years.

Holmefield
William Clegg (*1807-1897) was a cashier to a warehouse, born in Yorkshire. He and his family had lived in Stanley Grove for over twelve years, and in 1866 he bought a plot of land off Hope Road. Here he built four pairs of large semi-detached houses along a short road which he named 'Holmefield'. The Cleggs moved into the first house on the north side in 1868. William owned this pair of houses (numbers 1 and 3); the six houses on the south side belonged to William B. Clegg, possibly his son. The residents in 1871 were William Clegg himself, John Jones (a retired merchant born in Manchester in *1802), Thomas Worthington (a pawnbroker, born in Manchester in *1811), Alfred Firth (an oil merchant born in Northwich in *1826), Henry Taylor (a shipping clerk, born in Manchester in *1827), Lewis Auty (a grocer born in Dewsbury in *1832), Samuel Sedgeley (a merchant born in Worcester in *1832) and William Pearson (a stuff merchant born in Halifax in *1822). A further pair of houses (originally nos. 9 and 11, later numbered 5 and 7) were added on the north side in 1872. These were the homes of William Pollard (Secretary of the Peace Society, born in Horsham in *1829) and William Rylance (who moved here from Broad Road).

An unusual event occurred in Holmefield in 1871. A five year old boy ran out of one of the houses and jumped into a carriage waiting outside with such energy that the horse was terrified and bolted. It ran across Hope Road, through a hedge and on to the railway track, heading towards Manchester. Richard Wardleworth, the station master at Sale, managed to stop all the trains and eventually the horse, boy and carriage were rescued just north of the River Mersey.

(x) Wardle Road

Existing properties
During the period 1861-1876 the appearance of Wardle Road was drastically changed, as many new houses were built. There were naturally changes of ownership in the older properties. George Ollivant died in 1876, and his widow continued to live in the house. When J.K. Clough moved in 1876, his house was bought by James Forsyth, who had been living in 'Highfield' nearby; James (1831-1906) was a music publisher, born in London. He founded the music shop which still exists on Deansgate (Manchester), and was also one of the people who were instrumental in bringing the conductor Sir Charles Halle to Manchester. William Bridge, the owner of 'Moss Grove House' from 1851 moved into his house in 1863 and remained there until he died in 1896. 'Northern View' became the home of Martha Later in 1863. A widow born in Bowdon in *1803, she had been living in 'Marchfield Terrace'. She stayed in 'Northern View' for sixteen years. The adjoining house was the home of Robert Scott (1821-1892) for seven years from 1868. He was a land agent born in Cumberland. He owned a number of houses in Sale, and also the 'Brooklands Hotel'. The biggest change to existing properties took place when Thomas Renshaw at Wardle's Farm died in 1866; the old farmhouse was bought from the Denham family and rebuilt by William Thornber, who had been living further down Wardle Road. The new enlarged house was now 'Wardle House'; the stone gateposts still stand, although the house itself was demolished some years ago. William Thornber's former house was now the home of a Czech tailor, Cyril Kretchy, who was born in Moravia in *1823.

New properties - west side
The late 1860's saw a number of houses built on the west side of Wardle Road. The first to be completed was 'Belmont', built in 1866 next to Wardle Farm. This was owned by Robert Briggs, a cloth salesman born in Manchester in *1833. Next was a house built in 1867 between 'Heathfield' and 'Ebenezer House'. This was the home of John Williamson, a shipping agent born in Armagh (Ireland) in *1821. When John Williamson and his family to a new house built next door in 1877, their old house was bought by Sale's most famous inhabitant - James Prescott Joule, the internationally-known physicist. In the same year a pair of semi-detached houses was built on the corner of South Grove and Wardle Road. These were formerly numbered 44 and 46; they are now numbers 58 and 60. They were the homes of Frederick Midwinter (a porter from Wiltshire) and John Davies (a retired publican born in North Wales in *1809). In 1868 another house was completed, next to 'Ebenezer House'. This was 'Overdale' (number 14), the home of Thomas Fildes, a packing case manufacturer born in Manchester in *1829. Two other houses were built in the same year. John K. Clough had bought a patch of land behind his house. Here he built a pair of semi-detached houses, which he named 'Sunny Bank'. The tenants of the new houses were Matthew Miller and Hankinson Luke

(1842-1909). They were respectively a cotton manufacturer born in Manchester in *1845 and a master ironmonger born in Knutsford in *1843. 'Sunny Bank' later became nos. 4 and 6, Broomville, when a short road was laid out and further properties built. For some years the Rev. Edward Morris had owned a plot between 'Aroma Terrace' and 'Lime Place'. In 1869 he had a detached house built on the plot, naming it 'Shrewsbury House' (he was born near Shrewsbury). The resident for a number of years was Robert Lomas, a corn merchant born in Salford in *1819.

New properties - east side
From 1869 a number of large houses were built on the east side of Wardle Road. Most of them were built in the early 1870's, as other large houses were being built on Northenden Road. The earliest was 'The Elms', which was completed in 1869 for Joseph Ingram, a bank manager and Justice of the Peace born in Abram (near Wigan) in *1818. Six years later he moved to a house in Beaufort Road. 'Broomfield', and 'Mayfield' followed two years later. 'Broomfield' was the home of Benjamin Hime, a music seller born in Liverpool in *1796. After living in 'Broomfield' for three years the Hime family moved on; the house was then bought by Joseph Horner, who had been living in West Grove. 'Mayfield' was for three years the residence of Matthew Miller senior, a cotton manufacturer born in Ireland in *1812. Then it became the home of John Magson for more than twelve years. John Magson was another cotton manufacturer born in Halifax in *1837. Before moving to Wardle Road he and his family had lived in one of two houses which he owned in Hope Road.

The other houses were 'Norton Villa' and 'Fern Lea' (1874), and lastly 'Thornhill', 'Laurel Bank' and 'Leigh Lodge' (1875). 'Norton Villa' and 'Fern Lea' were semi-detached, as were 'Thornhill' and 'Laurel Bank'. All four were built and owned by Thomas Lamb (see p.57). A Greek, Evangelo Vassilopulo, lived in 'Norton Villa' for two years; he called it 'Hermopolis'. Then it became the home of Matthew Miller senior from 1876 to 1877. 'Fern Lea' was the home of William Walker, who moved there from Priory Road. Alfred Morris lived in 'Thornhill' and Francis Amos in 'Laurel Bank'. The latter was a cotton manufacturer born in Liverpool in *1840. 'Leigh Lodge' was the home of Richard Alston, who moved there from Hope Road. He was a master ironmonger, born in Devon in *1841. In 1876 another four houses were nearing completion on Wardle Road. These were 'Inglewood', 'Avenham', 'Woodlands' and 'Thornlea'. The last two were also owned by Thomas Lamb. Although many of these poperties have been replaced by modern blocks of flats, in many instances the old gate-posts bearing the name still stand.

Highfield
The road was laid out in the form of T. The first two houses were completed in 1869, each house consisting of two large semi-detached houses. 'Beech Villa'

and 'Birch Villa' had a number of tenants in succession. The houses are now nos. 19 and 21. The other pair of semis, which had no name, were the homes of William Scott and James Forsyth for four years from 1872. James Forsyth then moved round the corner to Wardle Road (see above). These houses are now nos. 48 and 50 in Highfield Avenue. The next pair of houses were completed in the summer of 1871. These were 'Oak Villa' and 'Rio Cottage' (now nos. 11 and 13, Highfield). The former was the home for over sixteen years of Charles Schiele, a commercial clerk born in Frankfurt in *1838, while 'Rio Cottage' was the home of William Baird for four years. The last pair of houses were 'Rose Lea' and 'Selbourne Lodge', completed in 1873. For the first five years Major Henry Hurst lived at 'Rose Lea'; 'Selbourne Lodge' was the home of Frederick Price, a coroner born in Standish in *1822. He and his family stayed there for more than fifteen years.

(xi) Montague Road

There was very little change in Montague Road during the period 1861-1876. The only new property was a cottage built in 1871 near the Independent Chapel for the chapel-keeper, Edward Williams, an army pensioner. William Critchley (*1822-88) and the widows of Joseph Fletcher and John Worthington continued to live in 'Brighton Place'. 'Albion Villa' was for a number of years the home of Mrs. Sarah Pendlebury, the widow of James who had lived in 'Strawberry Bank' (see p.44). She owned houses in Oak Road. In 1866 John Allen left 'Brookfield House'; the new tenant was Rebecca Kenworthy, a widow who stayed there for over ten years. 'Derby House' was now a school, run by Miss Sarah Barker, who came from London.

(xii) Poplar Grove

Mrs. Ellen Later continued to live in 'Moss Cottage' until 1870. Several tenants followed until 1874, when Ebenezer Lloyd Jones moved in from West Grove, where he had been living. A widower, he was a school-teacher, born in *1837 in Tenby (Pembrokeshire). In 1873 he started 'Brooklands School', a school for boys in a new building on Poplar Grove. The building survives, although it is now a driving test centre. Two of the inhabitants of Percival Terrace remained right through the years 1861-1876. These were Mrs. Mary Anderson and John Dutton. John Clarke also lived in no.21 for fourteen years from 1864. Other long-staying residents were Edmund Kerry, who moved into 'Northwood Lodge' (formerly 'Northwood Cottage') in 1869 and stayed for ten years (previously he had lived in 'Yew Villas' on Washway Road), and Joseph Hickin (*1801-72), who lived in 'Lime Villa' for ten years from 1868. He was a tax collector born in Staffordshire. One other resident of interest was Marmaduke Witty, who lived in 'Beech Villa' for five years from 1871. He later became well-known as the manager of the 'Moorfield Gardens'.

A terrace of four houses named 'Swiss Villas' was completed next to 'South Villas' in 1864. Originally nos.32 to 38, they are now nos. 40 to 46. The houses had a series of owners over the years. Two years later 'Northwood House' was built between 'Swiss Villas' and 'Northwood Lodge'. This was the home of Miss Hannah Booth, who was born in Yorkshire in *1839. She was a teacher, and probably taught in the boys' school up the road. On the south side of the road two pairs of semi-detached houses were built in 1868 and 1870. These were nos. 3 and 5, and nos.7 and 9. The first pair was owned by William Thornber (see p.52); the second pair (now nos. 9 and 11) were owned by one of the residents, Thomas Peacock, an office clerk born in Salford.

(xiii) South Grove

There was very little change in South Grove during the period 1861-1876. Mrs. Betty Derbyshire and Captain John Wight continued to live in nos.28 and 20 respectively right through the period 1861 to 1876. Other properties had several changes of residents. Only two new houses were built - numbers 2 and 4, completed in 1863. For ten years from 1866 no.4 was the home of Thomas Yates, the owner of the houses. He was an agricultural labourer born in Dunham near Altrincham in *1822.

(xiv) West Grove

The four houses existing in 1861 had a variety of tenants and owners in the years 1861-1876. Two new houses were built on the north side of West Grove in 1864. These were nos. 7 and 9, the homes of John Twigge and Emmanuel Street. The former was a traveller and the latter was a grocer born in Ashton-under-Lyne in *1830. In the same year building started on the south side of the road. The first houses were 'Zizinia's Villas' (nos.4 and 6) and 'Antonio's Villas' (nos.8 and 10). The origins of the unusual names has not yet been discovered. 'Bankfield House' (no.2) was built later, in 1867. The houses in West Grove seem to have had numerous residents in the period 1861-1876. Among the short-term residents were Andrew Hamilton (who later settled in Clarendon Road), Williamson Dunn (see p.71), Hankinson Luke (see p.66) and Ebenezer Lloyd Jones (see p.68). 'Green Bank' was completed in 1868 for Joseph Horner, a solicitor born in Wakefield in *1816. He was a partner in the firm of Gardner & Horner, of 45, Cross street, Manchester. He and his family stayed six years and then moved to a new house on Wardle Road. The new owner of 'Green Bank' was Thomas Tyson (*1825-82), who was well-known for his restaurant off Market Street in Manchester. An amateur cornet-player also, he was born in Manchester.

(xv) Derbyshire Road

William Foyster (Samuel Brooks's solicitor) moved into 'Holly Bank' from Montague Road in 1865. He and his family remained there until he died ten years later. William Wilson the architect built a new house, 'Harper Hill', in 1862. He moved into it from School Road, where he and his family had lived for twelve years. The house was demolished some years ago, but the stone gateposts bearing the name remain. Further development took place at the Northenden Road end of Derbyshire Road in 1872, when the six houses of Albert Road were built. There were a number of different residents in the first few years, but William Woolmore (managing clerk to a cotton manufacturer) stayed in 'Moss Bank' for over fourteen years from 1874. In 1873 a pair of large semi-detached houses was built on the corner of Derbyshire Road and Northenden Road. One house was in Derbyshire Road and this was 'Clairville', the home of Michael Tracey, (1835-1881). Three other detached houses were completed in 1876. These were 'Haworth House', the home of William Armstrong, a bookseller born in Manchester in *1826, 'Cavendish Villa', the home of Arthur McDougall (no details known), and 'Birch Lea', the home of Vincent Kilburn (also no details known). The last two houses were owned by John Keal (see p.103) and one of them ('Birch Lea') was situated round the corner in a new road named 'Trinity Road'.

(xvi) Washway Road

Llewelyn Hanmer and his family continued to live at 'Mayfield' until the end of 1861, when they moved elsewhere. The house was then occupied first by Frederick Baxter and then by Thomas Bird. The latter was a man of independent means born in Penrith in *1808. The two households living in 'Broadoaks' remained unchanged until 1871, when the Midwood family left. Richard Zahn remained there until he died in Ireland in 1875, and his widow Ann continued to live in the house.

During the years 1860 and 1862 a number of houses were built between the shops (near School Road) and Sibson Road. These were at first known as 'Sunnyside', 'Yew Villas', and 'Leamington Villas', although many of the houses were later re-named. 'Leamington Villas' were completed first (see p.53). 'Sunnyside' (number 21) was completed in 1862, and had a number of residents. 'Yew Villas' (also completed in 1862) covered numbers 23 to 33. Among the long-staying residents were Thomas Piggott, a merchant born in Yorkshire in *1821, Benjamin Howes, an East India merchant born in London in *1833, Joseph Sandbach and later his widow Amelia, and John H. Larmuth, a surgeon, who was born in Salford in *1834. The only house remaining today is number 23, now called 'Haddon Lodge'. Numbers 25 to 37 were demolished to make way for a large block of local government offices, 'Warbrick House'.

Samuel Roebuck died in 1865; his widow, Hannah, continued to live in 'Sale Bank' until her death nine years later. The house was then inherited by her son-in-law, William Brakespear, an architect born in London in *1819. He had married the Roebucks' daughter, Eliza, but she had died at the age of 39, nine months before her father. Later he married her younger sister, Sarah. William Brakespear was the designer of the 'Dome' Methodist Chapel in Bowdon.

John Jackson left the 'Vine' in 1866 and the new licensee was Richard Wright, who was born in Hollinhead near Oldham in *1832. In 1871 the number of shops on Washway Road belonging to the Birkenhead family doubled in number when the two sons of George Birkenhead took the shop next to their father's. William and John were florists and nurserymen, specialising in ferns.

(xvii) Roebuck Lane

The tenant of 'Sale Bank Cottage' for 8 years from 1864 was Thomas Standring, a commercial agent born in Manchester in *1830. A bachelor, he lived in the cottage with one servant. After being empty for two years, 'Green Bank' received its first residents in 1863. They were Abdullah Ydlibi in one half and Jane Binyon in the other. We have no further details about them, as they both moved on after a few years. One of the later residents was John Lilly, who lived in 'Green Bank' for twelve years from 1865. He was an 'African merchant', born in Manchester in *1829.

When Mrs. Ellen Ollier moved from 'Roseville Cottage' to Poplar Grove in 1862, her place was taken by William Jackson, a tea merchant born in York in *1832. The other half of the house was the home of Williamson Dunn, an auctioneer and valuer born in Blackburn in *1827. He moved out in 1864 and lived in several addresses in the centre of Sale, until he died on a visit to London in 1874. The next person to live in 'Roseville Cottage' was the owner, John Renshaw. He was a retired merchant born in Ashton-on-Mersey in *1801. He lived there until his death in 1875. William Jackson bought a plot of land next to 'Roseville Cottage' and built a pair of semi-detached houses on it in 1870. The first tenants were Edward Wilding (a wholesale stationer) and William Ashford (a commercial traveller).

One other house was built on Roebuck Lane in 1867. This was 'Bank Cottage', on the south side of the road. It was the home of William Houghton until 1870, and then of Thomas Sharples for ten years after that. We have no information about either man.

6. THE DEVELOPMENT OF NORTHERN SALE 1806-1876

The area covered by this chapter is bounded by the River Mersey on the north, Cross Street on the west, Chapel Road and Broad Road on the south, and Old Hall Road on the east. It includes part of Cross Street, all Dane Road, Broad Road (both sides), Priory Road and Clarendon Crescent (see map, p.30).

The Area in 1806

Two thirds of the area described in this chapter lies between Dane Road and the River Mersey. This area in particular was prone to frequent floods (one such occurred as recently as 1925), and seems to have been enclosed very gradually. Each time an area of land was enclosed, the existing landowners were allotted a portion. As the area in question was often some distance from existing farms, the result was a patch-work quilt of ownership, with each farm having its fields scattered and separated (unlike the south of Sale, where most farms had their fields adjacent to each other in large 'blocks'). This effect was heightened when Sale Moor was enclosed in 1806-7 and all landowners received a further portion of land (see p.11). The farms in the north were some distance from the Moor, and their allocated fields in the newly-enclosed area were half a mile or more from the rest of the farm.

(i) Cross Street

Cross Street was part of the old Roman Road from Chester to Manchester (see p.14). As already mentioned on page 31, it probably took its name from the cross which used to mark the ford (or ferry) over the River Mersey where Crossford Bridge now stands.

By 1806 there were six properties on the Sale side of Cross Street between Chapel Road and Dane Road. Going from Chapel Road towards Dane Road, the first property a traveller saw was a set of farm buildings owned by Joseph Atkinson, a Manchester hat-maker (see p.31). We don't actually know the name of the farm, but shall refer to it as 'Atkinson's Farm'. The farm was rented by Thomas Haslam, who lived there with his wife, Betty. The farmhouse still stands on Cross Street, where it is now usually referred to as 'Eyebrow Cottage', because of the shape of the brickwork above the windows. The farm itself included an orchard and eight fields (some on the south side of School Road), totalling 23 acres. Almost next door to the farmhouse was the Old Manor House, owned and occupied by John Moore (1751-1826), a wine-merchant with premises in Manchester. His family had lived on Cross Street for many years, and it seems that he obtained the Old Manor House by marrying into the Irlam family, who owned much of the land on the Sale side of Cross Street.

There were two houses south of the junction of Cross Street and Dane Road.

A widow, Rebecca Baker, owned two cottages some fifty yards south of the narrow junction (she lived in one of them) and right at the narrow junction itself were the house and shippen belonging to John Heald (*1749-1823). He also had two fields behind his house. Opposite, on the north side of the junction, there were seven cottages and beyond them, Manor Farm. Peter Heward (also written 'Heyward' or 'Heywood') owned both the cottages and the farm. He lived at the latter with his wife, Frances, and his farm fields were located on both sides of Dane Road. In addition to Manor Farm he owned Clark's Hey Farm, which was situated between the canal and Broad Road (see p.77).

(ii) Dane Road

Dane Road was an old road going back possibly to Saxon times. In 1806 it was called 'Dean Lane', meaning 'the road along the valley'. It actually ran along higher ground approximately 700 yards south of the Mersey, thus avoiding the land next to the river, which was often under several feet of floodwater.

The canal was crossed by means of 'White's Bridge', which in 1806 was only 12 or 13 feet wide. Immediately after crossing the bridge, a traveller would see White's Monument standing in the fields on the left. This was a stone column erected in 1790 in honour of the famous surgeon, Dr. Thomas White, by his son, Charles. The column finally collapsed in 1935, when a housing estate was being built round it. Dr. Thomas White (1696-1776) was one of the most famous surgeons in eighteenth-century England, and was one of the founders of Manchester Infirmary. He was also famous for his rather grisly museum which he kept in his house, 'Sale Priory'. The museum included the skeleton of Edward Higgins and the embalmed body of Hannah Beswick. Edward Higgins was a highwayman who had lived in Knutsford for about ten years before he fled south. He was hanged in Carmarthen Gaol in November, 1767. Hannah Beswick had died in 1758 and, according to one version of the story, she had asked that her body be kept above ground because of a fear of being buried alive. Another version says that Dr. White would receive a large amount of money in her will as long as she was kept above ground. This is not true; in her £25,000 will she left only £100 to Dr. White. Whatever his reasons were, Dr. White embalmed her body and kept it for a short period at his residence in King Street, Manchester, and then later at his Sale home, where it remained until the death of Dr. White's son Charles in 1813. When Charles White died, the body was bequeathed to his friend and colleague Dr. Thomas Ollier. After Dr. Ollier's death in 1832 Hannah's body was exhibited in the Manchester Museum of Natural History in Peter Street for a number of years. She was finally buried in 1868, 110 years after her death. 'Sale Priory' was never the home of a religious order, but was a large early Georgian mansion set in 5 acres of grounds nearly 400 yards along Dane Road from the monument. In 1806 Thomas White's son, Charles (1728-1813), was living at the house with his wife, Ann. Charles was also a doctor, and he owned nearly a sixth of the cultivable area of Sale (see p.20). Most of his land lay between the house and the River Mersey, but he also owned Sale New Hall to the east and Chadwick's Farm right on the southern boundary of Sale.

A large house stood on the south side of Dane Road, at the top of Priory Road. This was 'Miry Gate House', the home of John Leebridge, a widower who died later in 1806. The house and 42 acres of surrounding land was owned by the Earl of Stamford, and, as John Leebridge is described as being from 'Stayley', it seems that he had connections with the Earl of Stamford's other property in Stalybridge.

The area at the junction of the modern Arnesby Avenue and Dane Road was called 'Pepper Hill'. Here there were two farms, both belonging to the Earl of Stamford. The first was rented by Hannah Heyward, and covered 24 acres. The second, which was slightly larger, was leased to John Moore and another person named Irlam (probably his brother-in-law). Behind the farm buildings Cow Lane ran down through the meadows to the River Mersey. It survives today as an overgrown track running off Arnesby Avenue behind Mersey Court.

Further along Dane Road there were two cottages on the right-hand side of the road and a house on the left. The cottages were the home of Thomas Woodall and others; the house opposite them was rented with two fields by John Royle. The cottages were later enlarged and were finally demolished almost overnight in August, 1998. At the junction of Temple Road and Dane Road stood the Pinfold, an enclosure where stray animals were kept until reclaimed by their owners. Its situation points to the fact that the inhabitants of the time considered this junction to be near the centre of Sale. Facing the Pinfold was a farm which had been rented from Lord Stamford for over 25 years by Ashton Kelsall (*1740-1813) and his wife Martha. The farmhouse is still standing. Near Ashton Kelsall's Farm was another set of buildings - those of Dane Road Farm. In 1806 this comprised 30 acres and had been leased by George Woodall (*1760-1820) from J.G. Legh for over 20 years. The farmhouse is still occupied, although some of the farm buildings were demolished in a twentieth-century road-widening scheme.

At the junction of Dane Road and Old Hall Road there were two cottages - the homes of John Cookson and Edward Hampson (*1753-1830) - and a farm (35 acres), leased from Ralph Ashton by James Marsland (*1764-1824). James was the owner of another farm in the east of Sale (see p.117).

(iii) Priory Road

In 1806 Priory Road was called 'Miry Lane', presumably because of the prevailing conditions under foot. It contained three properties. The largest, 'Baxter's Farm' (or 'Priory Farm') was nearly opposite Miry Gate House; it covered 41 acres and belonged to Henry Baxter. It was rented by James Hulme, who also rented a second farm ('Pearson's Farm') on the other side of the road, halfway down towards Broad Road. James had run these two farms for over 25 years. The third property was a house and garden rented from the Earl of Stamford by Evan Royle (*1739-1819), who lived there with his wife,

Sarah. Abbot's Court now stands on the site.

(iv) Clarendon Crescent

Clarendon Crescent (known as 'Back Lane' until about 1867) ran roughly on its present alignment, but halfway along it forked into two. The land at the southern end belonged to Lady Jane Thorold, and on the east side of the fork was a 21-acre farm leased from her by Thomas Moore (*1736-1815), whose property included an orchard. The land at the northern end was owned by the Earl of Stamford, and in the fork itself was a house and garden leased by David Dickinson, who lived with his wife Elizabeth. 'Ivy Cottage' survives today, although it has been extended. Along the left fork (which is now a dirt track) was the small house and garden of Betty, the widow of Henry Pears. The land between the two forks is now Sale Cricket Club. The former landowner's name is remembered in 'Thorold Grove', a small cul-de-sac off Broad Road.

There were two other properties in the fields between Broad Road and Dane Road. One, consisting of two houses, was between Priory Road and Clarendon Crescent; the names of the occupiers are not known. They were probably labourers who worked for the farmer John Whitehead of Broad Lane, who is named as the occupier of both the houses and the fields round them. The other was a 22-acre farm between Clarendon Crescent and Temple Road, rented by Samuel Taylor and his wife Ellen. All three houses had disappeared by 1841.

(v) Temple Road north of Broad Road

The northern section of Temple Road was called 'Finch Lane' until 1867. The only buildings in 1806 were those of Temple Farm, which was situated at the north end, near the junction with Dane Road. The 23-acre farm was owned by Lord Stamford and run by Richard Knight and his wife, Ann.

(vi) Broad Road

Broad Lane, as Broad Road was called until 1867, originally ran from the crossroads at Four Lane Ends to the bottom of Priory Road ('Miry Lane'). It was lined by hedges, and the Enclosure Award describes it as an 'ancient highway'. There must have been some sort of path through to Sale Bridge to give access to the farm at Clark's Hey. The section between Priory Road and Sale Bridge was comparatively new in 1806. It had been shown with dotted lines on the Legh Estate map of 1801, but in 1807 it was described as 'newly formed and staked out'. It was now a road thirty feet wide, running just inside the northern edge of Sale Moor. The only building on Broad Road at this time was a farmhouse ('Broad Lane Farm') standing on the south side of the road, roughly halfway between Temple Road and Old Hall Road. The farm (44 acres) was owned by G.C. Legh, and was tenanted by John Whitehead (*1764-1838). Five of its eleven fields were situated behind the farmhouse, but most of the others were scattered over the Mersey flood plain. The house survives under a different name ('Barnwood') at the corner of Evesham Grove. In

'Yew Tree Cottage' (now 'Barnwood') on Broad Road was originally an old farmhouse. It dates back to the eighteenth century (see p.75)

1806 there was a large pond on the opposite side of the road.

There was another small farm set back between Broad Road and the canal. This was Clark's Hey; it consisted of 6 fields (8 acres) owned by Peter Heward of Manor Farm, and was tenanted by William Harrison.

1806-1841

(i) Cross Street

Thomas Haslam died around 1812, and his widow Betty ran Atkinson's Farm until Thomas Richardson (*1789-1865) took over in 1821. He was born in Sale and lived with his wife, Elizabeth. John Moore, the owner of the Old Manor House, purchased Sale Old Hall in 1807 and the Lordship of the Manor three years later (see p.121). The Old Manor House itself became a school in 1830 when Mrs. Jane Bellott leased the building. John Moore died in 1826 and he was succeeded by his son, 'John junior' (*1775-1857) (see also p.82). Peter Heward died in 1817 and Manor Farm was then run by his son Thomas until his death in 1843. In 1829 the house at the corner of Dane Road (formerly John Heald's) was bought by a joiner named Joseph Nield. Born in Chester in *1791 he lived there until his death in 1854.

(ii) Dane Road

Dr. Charles White of the Priory died in 1813 and his heir was his grandson, John (1791-1866). John was a captain in the North Derbyshire (High Peak) Yeomanry Cavalry. In 1829 he appears to have moved out and rented the 'Priory' to a succession of professional men who worked in Manchester (see p.148). One of these was John F. Foster (1795-1858), a magistrate who was born near Halifax in Yorkshire. He had chambers at 5, St. James's Square, Manchester, and he and his family rented the 'Priory' for about fourteen years from 1839. After the death of John Leebridge his son William lived at 'Miry Gate House' until 1814, and then the house was rented by various occupants. It was sold to Samuel Brooks, the Manchester banker, in 1828. Nine years later he leased it to his friend, John Brogden (1798-1869), although the latter appears not to have taken up residence until the early 1840's. Certainly the 1841 Directory of Manchester gives his address as 'Ardwick Green' and the 1841 census of Sale shows only the Cordingley family at 'Miry Gate'. Joseph Cordingley (*1803-1878) was a Northenden man who had married a Sale girl. Presumably he ran the farm for John Brogden until 1843, when he moved to Temple Farm. This is probably when the Brogdens took up residence at 'Miry Gate'.

Thomas Woodall's cottage was the home of John Carter from 1823. The latter was a cordwainer born in *1801. By the time of the 1841 census the cottage had been enlarged and was occupied by William Alderley (*1799-1863), a wheelwright born in Sale (John Carter having moved into a new house at Pepper Hill). John Royle's cottage was now the home of John Walkden, an agricultural labourer born in Sale in *1802.

Ashton Kelsall died in 1813 and the tenancy of his farm went to his son, James (*1766-1838), who bought the farm from Lord Stamford in 1828. James died ten years later, and the farm was sold off over the next six years, most of the land being bought by Samuel Brooks. The land leased by James Marsland

'Ivy Cottage' on Clarendon Crescent dates back to the eighteenth century (see p.75).

from Ralph Ashton was split up and sold when the owner died in 1810.

During the years 1828 to 1831 Lord Stamford sold many of his Sale properties to Samuel Brooks. Three of these were situated in the northern part of Sale and were sold in 1830. They were Temple Farm and the two farms at Pepper Hill. John Moore, however, continued to lease his farm from the new owner, and the Cookson family ran it from 1817 to 1849.

George Woodall left Dane Road Farm in 1812 and the tenancy was taken over by John Singleton (*1782-1862), who ran the farm until 1847. John was born in Sale and lived with his wife, Sarah.

By 1840 a coal wharf had been established at White's Bridge. The coalman was Joseph Whitelegg, who lived in a cottage on the east side of the bridge. At the same time James Brownhill had established a smithy and beer-selling business in a cottage on the west side of the bridge. Although the smithy was some distance from the turnpike road, it was next to the canal, and the barge horses must have provided a steady amount of work.

(iii) Priory Road

The two farms on either side of Priory Road changed hands several times. In 1825 Thomas Bancroft (*1757-1834) took over Baxter's Farm, and he stayed there fifteen years. During this time he enlarged Evan Royle's house, and the resulting three houses ('Bancroft's Houses') were occupied by his farm labourers. He was succeeded in 1840 by Peter Brown, who had been at Moor Nook Farm for fifteen years (see p.99). Peter (1798-1874) was born in Sale, and lived with his wife, Alice, and their three children. They had four 'servants' to help run the farm (presumably these acted as agricultural labourers). The tenancy of Pearson's Farm was given to John Hancock around 1834, and he remained there until 1847, when he moved to Washway Farm. He was born in Stretford in *1787.

(iv) Clarendon Crescent

During the years 1806-1841 the right-hand portion of Clarendon Crescent (between 'Ivy Cottage' and Dane Road) became disused and disappeared completely. Thomas Moore's farm also disappeared, the land being sold off in 1820.

(v) Temple Road north of Broad Road

Temple Farm had a number of tenants until the Barlows took over the tenancy in 1821. First Samuel (*1750-1823) ran the farm. He also had a small-holding near what became the 'Legh Arms' (see p.96). When he died, his widow, Alice, ran both until her retirement in 1830. Their son Thomas (*1798-1852) then took over as tenant of Temple Farm and in the same year, Lord Stamford sold the farm to Samuel Brooks, the Manchester banker. Thomas Barlow was a widower; his wife, Hannah, had died in 1829 at the early age of 27.

(vi) Broad Road

For fifty years the Wesleyan Methodists in Sale had met in private houses. However on 6th August, 1820, they opened a small new chapel on Broad Road - nearly opposite Broad Lane Farm. This was the first of many Methodist churches built in Ashton and Sale in the nineteeth century. Its position - at the opposite end of the parish to St. Martin's, the parish church - meant that many of the inhabitants of eastern Sale preferred to worship there as Methodists rather than walk nearly two miles to St. Martin's.

In 1824 Charles Jackson built a cottage on the south side of Broad Road between Clarendon Crescent and Temple Road. Charles (*1788-1862) was a gardener, born in Baguley. Clark's Hey Farm had a number of tenants during the years 1806 to 1826. John Sutherland (*1805-1875) took over the tenancy in 1827; he was born in Sale, and lived with his wife, Betty. They stayed at Clark's Hey until 1844.

When John Whitehead died in 1838, the tenancy of the farm on Broad Road devolved on his son, also named John. Nine years later he and his family moved to Manor Farm (see p.82).

1841-1861

A detailed description of the area and its inhabitants in 1841 is given in *Sale, Cheshire, 1841* (pages 30-31, 70-71 and 78-80).

(i) Cross Street

There was very little physical change to the area during the years 1841-1861. When Thomas Heward died in 1843 the tenancy of Manor Farm was handed to John Whitehead of Broad Lane Farm. He was born in Sale in *1797 and lived with his wife, Ann. They remained at Manor Farm until shortly before John's death in 1867.

The Old Manor House ceased to be a school when Jane Bellott retired to Bowdon in 1849. The occupant for six years from 1850 was Oswald Grundy, a shipping merchant born in Cheetham, Manchester. He and his wife had spent some time abroad, as four of their five young children had been born in Valparaiso, Chile. Soon after the Grundys moved out, John Moore, the owner of the Old Manor House and Old Sale Hall, died at his home in Cornbrook Terrace, Stretford. He was buried in St. Martin's Church in May, 1857, next to his wife, Sarah, who had predeceased him by 20 years. After the Grundys left, the Old Manor House became the home of Mrs. Mary Denman; then in 1859 it was rented by the Rev. Alfred Ellis, curate of St. Martin's Church, Ashton-on-Mersey. Around this time it was bought by William Ward (*1808-65), a painter and builder, who also bought 5 acres of land behind Atkinson's Farm at the same time.

Joseph Nield decided to build a row of houses next to his own house. The result was 'Mount Pleasant', a row of 8 houses completed in 1851. All except his original house were unoccupied at the time of the 1851 census, but they were soon all taken, mostly by professional people. One house became a school, run by Mrs. Mary Ann Bayley.

One of the tradesmen who moved into Cross Street around 1853 was George Ashcroft (*1816-86), a slater born in Sale.

(ii) Dane Road

By 1844 Mary Kelsall had sold Pinfold Farm to Samuel Brooks and Thomas Barlow. The latter rented his 12 acres to James Bardsley, who lived in the house on Dane Road. Dane Road Farm was also sold to Samuel Brooks in 1847; he incorporated it into Temple Farm, which he had bought from Lord Stamford seventeen years earlier. John Singleton retired and went to live in a house near the 'Guidepost' (the junction of Wythenshawe Road and Northenden Road).

In 1849 Samuel Brooks also bought a pair of large semi-detached houses behind the farms at Pepper Hill. This was 'Priory Bank', built two years earlier by John Whittenbury. The first tenants were William Southwell and William Swire. The latter was a director of the Dukinfield Coal Company, which had offices in Sale, on the Bridgewater Canal. In the 1851 census William Swire is described as a 'coal miner', but by 1861 he had become 'coal proprietor, partner in colliery and ironworks'. He and his wife Elizabeth had two servants. William Southwell was a merchant from Liverpool. He did not stay long at 'Priory Bank', and his house was bought by Alfred Milne, a barrister born in Salford in *1819. He lived with his wife, Ellen, four children, a governess, a cook, a nurse and a house servant. Samuel Swire continued to rent his house from Samuel Brooks.

By the time of the 1851 census there were three buildings on the west side of White's Bridge. One was still a smithy, the home of John Evans from Montgomery; the second was the home of John Dudley (*1804-1852), a gardener born in Nantwich (his name is commemorated by the nearby Dudley Road). Both of them had married local girls. From around 1855 the third house was the home of James Lawton Richardson (*1808-1864). James was born in Ashton-on-Mersey and he and his family had formerly lived on Cross Street; he now combined the three professions of insurance agent, auctioneer and beer-seller. His house later became the 'Bridge Inn'.

At the same time Joseph Whitelegg's house on the opposite side of the canal had disappeared. One of the two old farms at Pepper Hill had also disappeared, and the Cookson farm had been bought by John Whittenbury.

In 1851 John Carter's cottage at Pepper Hill was now the home of Thomas Dale, who was born in Manchester in *1816, and lived with his wife, Marianna. He was a builder, employing sixty men, and he probably enlarged the house and gave it its name ('Priory Cottage'). Six years later the Dales moved out and the house was occupied by John Arnold and his wife, Mary Ann. John was a wholesale grocer born in Yorkshire in *1814.

John Foster and his family left the 'Priory' some time between 1851 and 1856, and the next tenant was Gustavus C. Schutz, a merchant born in Holstein, Germany. He had married a girl from Worthing and had become a British subject. John Brogden continued to rent 'Miry Gate House' until 1859. Not being happy with the name 'Miry Gate House', he changed it to the more genteel-sounding 'Priory Gate House'; at the same time, 'Miry Lane' became 'Priory Lane', although the old names lingered on (the Rate Book for 1857 mentions 'Miry Gate House'). It appears that for some time 'Miry Gate House' was run as a farm for John Brogden by Joseph Cordingley (*1803-78), a farmer who was born in Northenden and who had married a girl from Sale. When John Brogden and his family moved into 'Miry Gate House' in 1843, the Cordingleys moved to Temple Farm. In 1859 John Brogden and family moved to a new house just off Washway Road (see p.102), and the new tenant of 'Priory Gate House' was John Herriot, an East India merchant, born in Scotland in *1817.

Henry Whitmore, a bookseller born in Manchester in *1815, moved into a house named 'Sale Green House' in 1849. Its exact location has proved impossible to ascertain despite a lengthy search through all relevant documents. The only time it is mentioned is in the 1851 census, where its position in the listing makes it very likely that it was the house later named 'Beechwood'.

(iii) Priory Road

The Browns continued to farm at Baxter's Farm. The neighbouring farm (Pearson's Farm) was now run by John Hancock, who moved to Washway Farm in 1847. The succeeding tenant was his son, Samuel, who hitherto had been living in one of Bancroft's Houses. Samuel in turn moved to Washway Farm when his father died in 1854, and he was succeeded at Pearson's Farm by John Ridyard, who in the following year married Samuel's daughter, Sarah. John was born at Walkden in *1836. He was the son of Richard Ridyard (see below).

(iv) Clarendon Crescent

The layout of Clarendon Crescent remained as before, with a sharp left turn at 'Ivy Cottage'. The latter was now the home of the Dunns and Stathams, families of market gardeners. By 1841 Betty Pears' house had become 'Priory Cottages', the home of several labourers who worked on one of the neighbouring farms.

(v) Temple Road north of Broad Lane

In 1843 Thomas Barlow left Temple Farm and took over the tenancy of the larger farm at Sale New Hall. His place at Temple Farm was taken by Joseph Cordingley who moved from Miry Gate Farm (see p.83). Generations of the Cordingley family stayed at Temple Farm until 1915.

(vi) Broad Road

In 1844 John Sutherland retired from Clark's Hey and went to live in one of the cottages at the top of Gratrix Lane. The tenancy of Clark's Hey was then given to William Smith (*1797-1875). He was born in Sale and lived with his wife, Martha. Before moving into Clark's Hey, they had lived in Jackson's cottage on Broad Road, so William had been a labourer at either Clark's Hey or possibly Broad Lane Farm.

A number of buildings were erected around 1855 on Wharf Road, a new road which led from Broad Road to the canal. The buildings were all owned by John Earl (see p.43) and included assembly rooms, a billiard hall, a school hall and five cottages. The cottages were called 'Woodland Cottages', because of they were near the wood at the junction of Broad Road and Northenden Road. Kelly's Directory for 1857 shows that the Assembly Rooms now housed a boys' school run by the Rev. George Slade.

Although John Whitehead had taken over the tenancy of Manor Farm in 1843, he continued at Broad Road Farm also, until 1847, when the latter was sold to Samuel Brooks. John and his family then moved to Manor Farm, and Broad Road Farm ceased to be a farm. It now became a large house ('Yew

Tree Cottage') in its own grounds. In 1851 it was the home of Joseph Barratt (a merchant, born in *1791 in Manchester), while from 1855 it was the home of George Horsfall, a merchant and wholesale grocer, born in Ravensfield (Yorkshire) in *1809.

Along Broad Road itself a number of large houses were built. First was 'Holly House', a very large property built in 1849 next to 'Yew Tree Cottage'. It stood in 2½ acres of grounds and had a lodge-house at the gate. From 1851 it was rented by Watson Losh, a calico printer from Carlisle. He lived with his wife, Martha (born in Portsmouth), his brother Dixon, and his sister-in-law, Harriet. In the 1861 census, we find that another (older) brother, John, had bought 'Holly House' and was living in it, Watson and his family having moved to Salford. The 1851 census lists another four new houses being built in 'Broad Road'. These were in fact situated at the north end of Clarendon Road, and are discussed on page 46.

In 1855 a large new house - 'Exeter House' was built for the Skaife family. William Skaife (1819-1879) was a 'salesman to a calico printer' with premises at 113, Dale Street, Chorlton-cum-Medlock. He was born in Braisty Wood (near Pateley Bridge in Yorkshire) and lived with his wife, Harriet, two of their children, and a niece. The family suffered several tragedies shortly after arriving in Sale. Two infant daughters were buried on the same day in November, 1856, and a third daughter (only two years old) was buried fourteen months later. The short track which led from Broad Road to the Skaifes' house later became Skaife Road.

By 1856 a medium-sized pair of semi-detached houses had been built on the north side of Broad Road. This was 'Beswick Place', set back from the road and next to the Methodist Chapel. It took its name from the owner - George Beswick, who died two years after the house was built. His widow, Mary, continued to live there until 1880. At the time of the 1861 census she had five daughters living with her. The other half of the house was occupied from 1859 by Edward Ratcliffe (*1825-1890). He was a cotton goods salesman, born at Bucklow Hill near Knutsford. Before moving to 'Beswick Place' he had lived in 'Renshaw Terrace', near the canal. Lastly, in 1859, a very large detached house was built on the south side of Broad Road, at the junction with Temple Road. This was 'Claydon House', which presumably took its name from the large house of that name in Buckinghamshire. Its namesake in Sale was not as grand, but was a large house standing in 3 acres of ground. It was the home of William Butterfield, a merchant born in Manchester in *1802. His wife Elizabeth was born in Altrincham. Before moving to 'Claydon House', they had lived on Clarendon Road for a few years. Prior to that they lived on Hyde Road, Manchester. They had four children, two servants and a groom.

A smithy had stood for many years near the corner of Broad Road and Old Hall Road. From 1855 this was rented by William Yarwood (*1839-1890). Born in Northenden, he moved with his family from Broadheath to Sale. The 1861 census shows him living with his wife, Sarah, one daughter, his grandfather (also a blacksmith), a brother and a sister, in one of the cottages opposite the 'Jolly Carter' on Northenden Road.

1861-1876

(i) Cross Street

In 1863 William Ward, the owner of the Old Manor House, started to build another house on the land he had bought behind Atkinson's Farm ('Eyebrow Cottage'). The entrance to the new house lay between the farmhouse and the Old Manor House. The new house was named 'Grove House' but unfortunately William Ward died in 1865 soon after the house was completed. His widow, Ann, continued to live there until her death 12 years later. When the Rev. Ellis left the Old Manor House it was then let to Mrs. Ellen Ogden, a veterinary surgeon's widow with a private income; she was born in Manchester in *1812. She stayed in the house for 11 years. It was now called 'Summerville', although the old name was revived towards the end of the nineteenth century.

The farm next door ('Atkinson's Farm') was run by Thomas Richardson until his death in 1865. From 1871 it was rented by Thomas Lee, although it is probable that he had already run the farm for six years. He was born in Irlam in *1835, and he lived with his wife, Anne Jane. When John Whitehead died in 1867, Manor Farm was rented from the Heywards by John Worthington. He and his family lived there for eight years, and during this period it appears that he did not run the farm, as the 1871 census gives his occupation as 'merchant'. It seems probable that Thomas Lee managed Manor Farm at this time as Atkinson's Farm had by now shrunk to almost nothing.

New properties

Two new streets were built between 1861 and 1876, both at right angles to Cross Street itself. The first one, built in 1867, consisted of two terraces of four houses and three pairs of semi-detached ones, all on the south-west side of the road, facing the River Mersey. The street was named 'Hesketh Road', taking its name from the owner, Peter Hesketh, who at one time lived nearby in 'Mount Pleasant'. The two terraces survive today. The other street was King Street, a street of 11 terraced houses built four years later near the four shops which had been completed in the previous year next to the junction with Chapel Road.

(ii) Dane Road

There were very few changes on Dane Road during the period 1861 to 1876. Margaret Richardson continued to sell beer at the 'Bridge Inn' until her retirement in 1875. 'Priory Gate House' was rented by Isaac Hoyle for a number of years. He was a cotton manufacturer, born in Bacup in *1828. For many years Captain John White and his wife, Ellen, had lived not at 'Sale Priory' but at Park Hall near Glossop. During this time, 'Sale Priory' was rented to various wealthy professional men, and this continued after Capt. White's death at Northwich in February, 1866. The tenant of the 'Priory' for twelve years from 1866 was William Richardson Jolly, a merchant, born in Scotland in *1830.

Samuel Swire left 'Priory Bank' in 1863, and this part of the house then had a number of tenants; it also lay empty for some years. Alfred Milne sold his house back to Samuel Brooks' executors in 1865. Three years later he moved, and the new tenant was Mrs. Martha Dale, a widow. 'Priory Cottage' was now 'Harwood House'; it was the home of Mrs. Elizabeth Cheetham, another widow, for six years from 1866. She then moved to Woodlands Road.

As already mentioned, from 1847 Dane Road Farm had been absorbed into Temple Farm. In the meantime the old house on Dane Road had several residents, including a widow, Mrs. Goodfellow, who took in lodgers. She lived in the house for over twenty years from 1862. The neighbouring Pinfold Farm was rented by James Hampson in 1861.

Some of the land near White's Bridge had been bought from John White by Samuel Brooks. Around 1860 a 'Hunting Establishment' was set up on this land, consisting of a cottage and stables run by William Murray. In 1866 he enlarged his establishment by taking over the buildings of a 'chemical works' which had been built next door two years previously. Owned by Samuel Brooks and run by G. Barnes, it must have been the first evidence of industry in Sale. Luke Winstanley, the Sale builder, established a brickworks on Dane Road in the late 1860's.

(iii) Priory Road

Priory Farm continued to be run by Peter Brown right up to his death in the summer of 1874. His widow, Alice, then took over. Generations of the Brown family ran the farm until 1929. The other farm on the opposite side of Priory Road was tenanted by John Ridyard until 1863, when Charles Morgan succeeded him. Charles (*1840-1913) was one of the six sons of Joseph Morgan, who farmed at Gratrix's Farm on Wythenshawe Road.

New properties
During the period 1868 to 1872 a number of houses were built on the east side of Priory Road, between the Bancroft houses and Broad Road. 'Ryburn Villas' (now numbers 8 and 10) were built in 1868 for Henry Shaw and John Robson. Henry Shaw was a clerk, born in Yorkshire in *1834; John Robson was a warehouseman, also born in Yorkshire, in *1835. 'Banana Villas' (now numbers 12 and 14) were built in the following year for John Brown and Benjamin Parr. John Brown soon moved to a larger house on Broad Road (see p.90); Benjamin Parr was a commission agent, born in Yorkshire in *1832. 'Priory Villa' (number 16) was built in 1870, and was the home of Denis Hallott. 'Fernlea' (also 1870) was the home of William Walker, who had been living in Temple Road. Four years later he moved again, this time to a new house on Wardle Road. 'Priory Mount' is a large house at the corner of Priory Road and Broad Road. The land it stands on was bought in 1871 by Peter Potts, a baker, who moved into one half of the house when it was completed in 1872. Previously he had lived with his family near the 'Lindow Tavern'. The other half of 'Priory

Mount' was the home of Henry Butterworth (*1818-94), a calico printer, born in Lancashire. The gap between 'Ryburn Villas' and 'Priory Mount' was filled in 1876 by the building of a pair of semi-detached houses. These were named 'Thornfield'and 'Beechfield'. The first residents were Mrs. Dowson (a widow of independent means born in Scotland) and John Hesketh (a salesman born in *1850 in Ashton-on-Mersey).

(iv) Clarendon Crescent
There were no changes in the layout of Clarendon Crescent. The road still had a sharp left bend near 'Ivy Cottage'. 'Priory Cottages' now housed Charles Fisher (a farm manager), John Burgess (a gardener) and John Wellford (a coachman).

(v) Temple Road north of Broad Road
The Cordingley family continued to farm at Temple Farm.

(vi) Broad Road
Existing properties
William Smith continued to farm at Clark's Hey until his death in 1875. Mrs. Beswick continued to live at 'Beswick Place' and the Skaife family still lived at 'Exeter House' until after 1876. 'Holly House' remained the property of the Losh family after John's death in 1872. 'Claydon House' however had several changes of ownership when the Butterfields moved out in 1869. It was finally bought by William Grimshaw in 1875 and re-named 'Stoneleigh'. The Grimshaws remained there for over thirteen years.

George Horsfall sold 'Yew Tree Cottage' to Vernon Cochrane in 1865. The latter was an East India merchant, born in Ireland in *1834. He and his family remained there for nine years. In 1862 'Beechwood' (at the corner of Broad Road and Old Hall Road) became the home of John Underwood and his family. He was a rope manufacturer, born in Salford in *1828. They moved to 'Lynwood Villas' in 1871 and the new resident of 'Beechwood' was Joseph Thorpe, a merchant born in Manchester in *1828.

New properties - north side
Since the north-western end of Broad Road was very near to Sale station, it was a prime site for development. 'Woodley Bank' (two semi-detached houses) was built in 1864. It was owned by Thomas Kirtley, who also owned the assembly-rooms, schoolhouse, mission rooms and cottages nearby. The residents of 'Woodley Bank' were Thomas Kirtley himself and Douglas Noble (*1823-79, a cashier and stationer, born in Scotland). The site of the houses later became a do-it-yourself store. Development in the area started apace in 1868 when Wharf Road, Bank Street and Brook Street were laid out. Building continued for nearly two years, and when completed these streets contained 56 terraced houses.

In 1869 a pair of semi-detached houses was built facing down Irlam Road, which was in the process of being laid out. The houses were named 'Irlam View', now numbers 17 and 19, Broad Road. The houses had a series of owners over the years. In the following year two more houses were built near 'Woodley Bank'. These were 'Stowey' and 'Gosport Villa'. They are now joined together and form the 'Belfort Hotel', but originally they were completely separate. The original owner of 'Stowey' was Robert Roberts, a slate merchant, but he moved out in 1873 and the house remained empty for several years. 'Gosport Villa' was built by Edward Parrish, a timber merchant born in Lincolnshire in *1830. He also soon moved (to Chapel Road) and the house was bought by Robert Ainsworth, a retired warehouseman born in Bury in *1803.

Also in 1869 a very large house ('Moorlands') was built at the corner of Broad Road and Clarendon Road, opposite 'Claydon House'. It stood in nearly 1½ acres of ground, and for several years was the home of William Rylance and his family. William Rylance (1834-1903) was a solicitor and attorney, born in Manchester. He had an office in King Street, Manchester. While 'Moorlands' was being built, he and his family had rented John Warriner's house in Warrener Street. When the Rylances moved to Holmefield in 1872, 'Moorlands' was bought by John Kendall, who had been living in 'Ellan Brook' on Brooklands Road. John Kendall was a merchant born in Lancaster in *1835. He and his family lived in 'Moorlands' for over 16 years.

One other house, 'Riversdale', was built at the corner of Priory Road in 1873. It was built for John Brown, who had been living in 'Banana Villas' in Priory Road. John Brown was a traveller, born in Manchester in *1842. He and his family lived in 'Riversdale' for twenty years. Another stage of development took place in 1876, when more houses were built on the north side of Broad Road. Luke Winstanley built two identical pairs of large semi-detached houses next to 'Riversdale'. The first pair were called 'Winterholme', and consisted of a house and a boarding-school run by Miss Louisa Milne. She had three teachers (two of them were her sisters) and four servants to help run the school. The second pair were 'South Bank' and 'Audley House'. The latter is now a Rest Home for the Elderly. 'Thornfield' and 'Greystoke' were very large semi-detached houses built in 1876 between Priory Road and Clarendon Crescent. The choice of the name 'Thornfield' seems strange when another 'Thornfield' was being built at the very same time round the corner in Priory Road.

New properties - south side
'Oak House' was built near 'Exeter House' in 1861. For 13 years it was the home of John Smith and his family. He was a chief cashier for a railway company, and was born in Manchester in *1816. The Jackson family built 14 cottages in 1867 near their own house. At first these were referred to as 'North View', but within ten years they became 'Jackson Street'. The street still exists

today, although all the old houses have been replaced by modern dwellings.

Another house, 'Lynwood Villas', was completed in 1870 at the corner of Irlam Road and Broad Road. For many years one half was the home of John Roberts, a bachelor. He was a commission agent, born in Yorkshire in *1817; the other half of the house had a series of owners. 'Lynwood Villas' are now numbers 18-20 Broad Road. Near 'Lynwood Villas' a nursery was established, belonging to Alex Pettigrew. The first mention of Sale Cricket Club occurs in the rate book for 1874, when the ground is listed. Both this and the 1888 Street Directory place the original ground at the corner of Broad Road and Clarendon Crescent.

Irlam Road

Four pairs of large semi-detached houses were built along the west side in 1870. These were nos. 7 to 21. The residents in 1871 were Augustus Warrens (a cotton spinner born in Sweden), Christopher Thistlethwaite (an estate agent), Mark Towler (a tailor and draper), Robert Parkinson (a retired cotton spinner), Francis Corkill (a man of independent means) and Thomas Quinn (a doctor of law). Two houses were still unoccupied.

In 1872 there was further development on Irlam Road when a large semi-detached house was built on the corner of Northenden Road. One of the houses was in Northenden Road and the other, 'Claremont', was in Irlam Road. 'Claremont' was the home of James Lynde, a civil engineer born in London in *1844.

Woodlands Road

Until about 1870 the triangle of land between Woodlands Road and Sale Bridge had been a wood, hence the name 'Woodlands Road'. However the first two houses in Woodlands Road were built in 1872 on the east side. These were two large semi-detached houses now numbers 12 and 14. The original residents were Charles Watson and Charles Platt. We have no details about them.

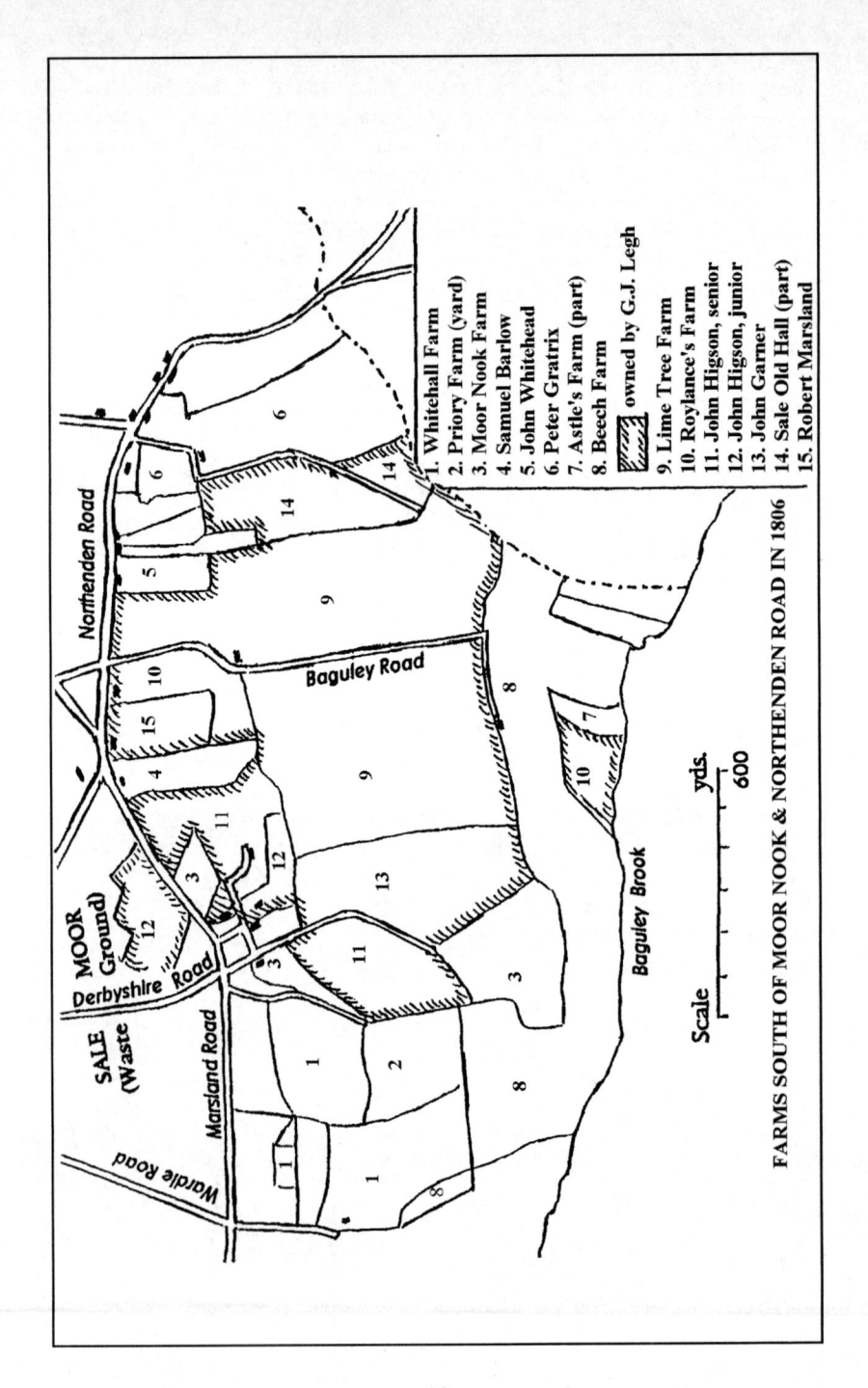

1. Whitehall Farm
2. Priory Farm (yard)
3. Moor Nook Farm
4. Samuel Barlow
5. John Whitehead
6. Peter Gratrix
7. Astle's Farm (part)
8. Beech Farm
   owned by G.J. Legh
9. Lime Tree Farm
10. Roylance's Farm
11. John Higson, senior
12. John Higson, junior
13. John Garner
14. Sale Old Hall (part)
15. Robert Marsland

FARMS SOUTH OF MOOR NOOK & NORTHENDEN ROAD IN 1806

7. THE DEVELOPMENT OF SOUTHERN SALE 1806-1876

This chapter covers the area south of Marsland Road. It includes Brooklands Road, Whitehall Road, Moor Nook, both sides of Marsland Road and the Sale side of Washway Road (see map, p.30).

The Area in 1806

The area south of Marsland Road was comprised of a number of large farms, most of which had been established for many years.In contrast to the farms in the north part of Sale, where each farm's fields were scattered over a large area, the farms south of Marsland Road seem to have been created as large units. Marsland Road ran along the southern edge of Sale Moor (see below).

(i) Washway Road

Washway Road was the old Roman Road from Chester to Manchester (see p.14). It was not developed until the 1950's; in 1806 therefore fields and hedges stretched on either side as far as the eye could see. There were a few farms and houses dotted here and there, and the first of these on a journey northwards from the Sale boundary at Baguley Brook was Washway Farm. This covered 64 acres, and was leased from the Earl of Stamford by Edward Pearson. 530 yards north was another farm; this was really part of the Riddings Hall Estate, owned by Joseph Taylor, and was rented by Joseph Goodier. There were no farm buildings until it became a separate entity at a later date with the name 'New Farm'. The shape of the farm shows that it was in existence before the cutting of the Bridgewater Canal in 1765-6.

160 yards from New Farm, Thomas Moss (*1761-1831), a tailor, lived with his wife Sarah. North of his cottage there was a large pond and beyond the pond a short track ran along the line of the later Raglan Road, turning south on the other side of the pond. This was 'Sale Heys Road' but is now merely a track leading behind the Baptist Church and the Peugeot Garage. The pond was the remains of a huge gravel or marl pit, which gave the surrounding area its name - 'Big Pit' or just 'Pit'. The track led to 'Sale Heys' (or 'Sale Heys Cottage'), a white-washed house where John Whitehead (?1767-1830) and his wife Mary had lived for over twenty-five years. Their house was also rented from Mrs. Taylor.

Back on Washway Road, John Howard lived in a house situated just to the north of the track and rented from Lord Stamford. Beyond his house Sale Moor stretched 800 yards almost to the modern Sibson Road (see p.11).

(ii) Marsland Road (west of Derbyshire Road)

There were no buildings on the north side of Marsland Road in 1806, as the Moor extended northwards from Marsland Road to the other side of

These houses on Marsland Road were originally, from left to right, 'Birch Cottage', 'Dunham View', 'Bowdon View' and (set back) 'Park View' (see p.103).

Northenden Road (see map p.10). Marsland Road ran just inside the southern edge of Sale Moor and had only recently been made into a proper road (see below). According to the Legh Estate map of 1801, at that time it took a more northerly direction on the west of the canal, meeting Washway Road opposite the end of Barker's Lane. It was originally 'Marsland's Road', taking its name from the Marsland family, who rented a farm south of the bridge over the canal (then 'Marsland's Bridge', now 'Brooklands Bridge'). The farm was the largest in Sale, covering 135 acres. In 1806 it was rented from Lawrence Wright by Edward Marsland (1765-1818), whose family had lived here for well over twenty-five years. Edward lived with his wife, Ann. The shape of the farm reveals that it was there when the Canal was cut. The farm was approached by a track and narrow bridge over the Fleam. On the north side of this bridge there was a much smaller farm. This comprised seven fields - 8½ acres in total - and was rented from Lord Stamford by James Kelsall (*1766-1838), the eldest son of Ashton Kelsall. Finally, nearer to Marsland Road was a smaller house still. This was the township poor-house. It is interesting to note that the poor were banished to an area well away from the majority of the population.

440 yards further to the east, Marsland Road was crossed by a road which led south across the Moor from Northenden Road. At a later date this would become Wardle Road (on the left) and George's Road (on the right), but in 1806 both were called 'Moss's Lane'. The name arose from the fact that the road led to Whitehall Farm, the home of John Moss (*1759-1819) and his wife Ann. The farm (12 acres) belonged to Lord Stamford, who leased it to William Williamson of Ashton New Hall. The Williamsons also owned 20 acres of adjoining land, which increased the farm's area. The farm was known for many years locally as 'Williamson's Farm' and the farmhouse still stands today near Brooklands Cricket Club on Whitehall Road. It is now a nursery school.

(iii) Moor Nook

At Moor Nook, 600 yards from Wardle Road, another road crossed Marsland Road. This was the road leading across the Moor from Northenden Road to 'Higson's Corner', as Moor Nook was called at the time. Here there were four farms and a number of cottages. The first property on the west side of the road was Moor Nook Farm (20 acres), rented from George Ashton by John Davenport. On the other side of the road were four cottages and three farms, the latter being run by John Garner (*1753-1838), John Higson senior (*1732-1814) and the latter's son, John Higson junior. The farms were leased from G.J. Legh, but John Garner owned his four cottages himself. The fields leased by these men covered 21 acres (John Garner), 28 acres (John Higson senior) and 11 acres (John Higson junior) (see map, p.92).

(iv) Marsland Road (east of Derbyshire Road)

From Moor Nook to the Legh Arms there were fields on the right and waste ground on the left, although some of this waste ground had been enclosed by

1806. This part of Marsland Road was called 'New Lane' until 1867, the name revealing the comparatively late origin of the road to Marsland's Farm. A farmhouse stood near the junction of Marsland Road and Northenden Road, where today a row of shops stands back at the end of Conway Road. This was the home of Samuel Barlow (*1750-1823) and his wife Alice. Samuel owned his own house and also the six acres behind the house which he cultivated.

There were two large farms to the south and east of Moor Nook - Lime Tree Farm (119 acres) and Chadwick's Farm (67 acres). As they extended eastwards beyond Baguley Lane they are both described in the next chapter ('Eastern Sale').

1806-1841

(i) Washway Road

During the period 1806 to 1841 there was very little change along Washway Road. The enclosure of Sale Moor in 1807 affected the area between Raglan Road and Marsland Road, and the area on both sides of Marsland Road. However many of the farms in the area were able to add fields which were contiguous to their existing farms.

In 1822 Joseph Hampson moved into Washway Farm with his wife, Deborah. They stayed there for over 20 years, although the farm changed ownership in 1828, when it was sold by Lord Stamford to Joseph Clark. New Farm possibly became a separate farm when Richard Haworth took over the tenancy in 1823. Richard remained there until his death nineteen years later.

In 1829 James Hamnett took over the lease of John Howard's cottage and garden just north of Raglan Road. Lord Stamford sold the property around 1830, and Samuel Brooks became James Hamnett's new landlord. James (*1792-1852) was born in Ashton-on-Mersey and lived with his wife, Ann. John Whitehead of 'Sale Heys Cottage' died in 1830 and the house saw a number of tenants over the next few years (see p.147). In 1838 Richard Yates (*1806-90), a confectioner born in Manchester, leased five fields at the end of Sale Heys Road from the executors of Joseph Clark. Here he built a house and established a nursery which supplied fruit and vegetables to his shop at 3, St. Ann's Square (Manchester).

(ii) Marsland Road (west of Derbyshire Road)

When Ashton Kelsall died in 1813 his eldest son, James, moved from the small farm near Brooklands Bridge to the larger one at the Pinfold. His younger brother, John (*1787-1859), then took over the smaller farm.

Edward Marsland died in 1818; the tenancy of the farm remained in the family, as it was taken over by Edward's son, Robert (1797-1867). We find him in 1841 living with his first wife, Sarah, and two children. His mother was now accommodated in a new house at the corner of Wardle Road (see p.37).

Lord Stamford had sold his share of Whitehall Farm to Samuel Brooks by 1831, but the dual nature of the farm continued, as the other half was inherited from the Williamsons by the Rev. John Hunter, the curate at St. Martin's. From 1827 the farm was tenanted by Thomas Renshaw, who moved here from Roylance's Farm on Northenden Road.

Around 1840 a small cottage - 'Moor Cottage' - was built on the north side of Marsland Road near the corner of Derbyshire Road. This and 5 acres of adjoining land ('Moorside Nurseries') were owned by Joseph Moore and occupied by James Bardsley, who also managed the Pinfold Farm. James (*1784-1856) was born in Sale.

'Woodheys' on Washway Road was built by Samuel Brooks in 1857 (see p.101).

(iii) Moor Nook

The farms at Moor Nook experienced changes of ownership and tenancy. Moor Nook Farm continued to be farmed by John Davenport until 1819. He was then succeeded by Samuel Davenport (his son?), who remained there for four years. In 1823 George Brown took over and he stayed there eighteen years. George Brown (*1772-1848) was born in Sale and lived with his wife, Margaret. There is some evidence that originally his name was 'Brownell' or 'Brownhill'. John Higson junior died in 1806. His farm continued to rented by successive members of his family until James Higson (his brother?) took over in 1827. James (*1794-1865) was the son of John, senior. The latter died in 1814, and his farm, which was on a long-term lease, was rented out to George Brown from 1821 to 1825. One of George's sons, Peter, then took over the tenancy until 1840, when he moved to Priory Farm. John Garner's Farm disappeared, being added to Moor Nook Farm, although the Garner family retained ownership of the cottages. By 1831 the number of cottages had grown to six and five years later there were nine.

(iv) Marsland Road (east of Derbyshire Road)

When Samuel Barlow died in 1823 his widow Alice continued to run the small-holding. She died in 1832, and in 1841 we find Samuel Woodall (1808-1893) in residence, living with his wife, Mary.

Joseph Moore built another house in 1840 on the north side of Marsland Road half way between Derbyshire Road and the junction with Northenden Road. The resident in the 1841 census was William Bardsley.

'Raglan House' was completed in 1859 by Joseph Thompson. The first residents were John Brogden and his family (see p.102).

1841-1861

A detailed picture of the area and its inhabitants in 1841 is given in *Sale, Cheshire, in 1841*, pages 22-25 and 55-58.

(i) Washway Road

During the twenty years from 1841 to 1861 there was little change in the south of Sale. Farms and properties changed hands, as might be expected, and a small number of new houses were built. When Richard Haworth died, his widow Martha continued to run New Farm for 2½ years, until John Carter took over the tenancy in 1845. John was born in Baguley in *1797; his wife, Sarah, was a Sale girl. John ran the farm for ten years; he was followed by Thomas Whitelegg, who was born in Ashton-on-Mersey in *1828 and lived with his wife, Esther. Washway Farm changed hands in 1847 when Joseph Hampson decided to leave and take a shop on Cross Street. His successor was John Hancock (from Pearson's Farm on Priory Road), who in turn was followed on his death in 1854 by his son, Samuel. The latter was born in Stretford in *1818, and he lived with his wife, Mary.

In 1842 part of the land of New Farm was purchased by Richard Lane (*1795-1858). Born in London, he was well-known in Manchester as an architect and surveyor. On the plot he built a large house - 'Beechfield' - where he lived with his wife, Emma, until his death. Both Richard and his wife were born in London. His works included Salford Town Hall, the Corn Exchange (Manchester), the Friends' Meeting House in Mount Street (Manchester), the dome and facade of Manchester Infirmary and Henshaw's Blind Asylum (Old Trafford), plus many local churches.

'Sale Heys Cottage' appears to have been enlarged around this time, and the tenant for twenty years from 1845 was David Bellhouse, a well-known builder, born in Manchester in 1792. His company was one of the five largest building companies in Britain. He employed 500 men and among his successful projects was the building of the short section of the Manchester, South Junction & Altrincham Railway between London Road (now Piccadilly) station and Ordsall Lane Junction in Salford (see p.28). Other buildings built by his company were the Theatre Royal, the first Manchester Town Hall, the City Art Gallery, the Gaol, and the warehouses of the Liverpool & Manchester Railway in Liverpool Road. A keen amateur singer, he was a founder member of the Manchester Choral Society. He lived at 'Sale Heys' until his death in 1866. Other members of his family came to live in Sale in the ensuing years including one of his younger brothers, John (*1798-1863), who bought 'Beechfield' when Richard Lane died. John Bellhouse was a timber merchant born in Manchester.

In 1856 Samuel Brooks bought part of one of the fields of New Farm from the owner, James Taylor. On it he built an extremely large house, which he called 'Woodheys'. He rented it out to John Critchley, a director of Critchley,

Armstrong & Co., silk manufacturers. Born in Manchester in *1824, he lived with his wife, Annie Jane. They had four servants to run the house, which is now a private sports club. Further to the north a builder by the name of Joseph Thompson built two houses on Raglan Road in 1858-9. Joseph (1807-88), who was born in Bishop Auckland, lived in one of the houses which he named 'Hope Cottage'. The second and larger of the two houses was leased by John Brogden, who moved from 'Priory Gate House' in 1859. He named his new house 'Raglan House', taking the name he had given to the house he had bought at Moor Nook (see p.105). In 1861 we find John Brogden living with his wife, Sarah, three of their children (including 33-year old Henry, an 'iron master') and three servants. The two houses survive today; 'Hope Cottage' is now a private school ('Southfields') and 'Raglan House' is divided into flats.

When James Hamnett died in 1852, his widow, Ann, continued with the smallholding until she died seven years later. From 1860 the tenancy was given to John Hockenhull, who was born in Ashton-under-Lyne in *1838. By renting neighbouring fields he expanded his nursery to 9 acres, and it became well-known in Sale in the 1860's and 1870's.

(ii) Marsland Road (west of Derbyshire Road)

Existing properties
Robert Marsland continued to farm at Wright's (Brooklands) Farm. His first wife, Sarah, died in 1843 and he took a second wife, Mary. In 1857 he retired to Bowdon, and the farm was taken over by Robert Cookson. The latter was born in Stretford in *1835, and lived with his wife, Mary. On the farm he employed 8 labourers and 2 boys. The Kelsall small-holding next door had ceased to be viable, as John gave his occupation as 'launderer' in the 1851 census. After his death in 1859 his widow, Sarah, continued the business.

Williamson's Farm had a new tenant in 1854; Peter Wardle (the tenant of Wardle's Farm on Wardle Road) died and Thomas Renshaw moved with his second wife Maria from Williamson's Farm to Wardle's Farm. His place at the former was taken first by William Bridge (the son of the owner of 'Moss Grove Cottage') and then by Richard Hayman, a cattle dealer born in Manchester in *1810.

James Bardsley died in 1856 and the tenancy of Moorside Nurseries was taken by James Alcock, who was born in Gatley in *1810. He and his son William rented the nurseries for over thirty years.

New properties - north side
A house was built between Washway Road and the canal in 1849. Owned by William Atkinson, who lived nearby in Sale Terrace, it was rented first by Andrew Howarth (a veterinary surgeon) and then from c.1853 by John Johnson (*1811-1874), a corn dealer's agent born in Manchester. The house was named 'Hope Cottage', and is still lived in today. It should not be confused with Joseph Thompson's 'Hope Cottage', which was built nine years later a little over

300 yards away down Washway Road (see above).
A number of houses were also built between Wardle Road and the modern West Grove. These were 'Vernon Lodge' (1851), 'Bowdon View' and 'Park View' (1856) and 'Dunham View' and 'Birch Cottage' (1859). These properties housed a number of professional people, most of whom had one or two servants. Some of them are now converted into shops (part of 'Bowdon View' is a beauty parlour). Peter Royle, a surgeon, had bought a plot of land at the junction of Northenden Road and West Grove. On it he built his own house ('Vernon Lodge'), another house ('Rose Villa' on West Grove) and two small cottages in South Grove. Born in Manchester in *1818, he lived with his Devon-born wife, Marianne, five children and two servants. His surgery was at 27, Lever Street, Manchester. 'Birch Cottage' was the home of Mary Denman, a widow from Ruthin in North Wales. Before moving to 'Birch Cottage' she rented the Old Manor House on Cross Street for two years.

New properties - south side
A number of houses were built on Marsland Road during the years 1841 to 1861. In 1848 William Prince (*1800-1879) bought a plot of land on the south side between Moor Nook and the track which later became 'Beaufort Road'. Here he built a house, where he lived with his wife and six children. William was a retired grocer, born in Youlgreave (Derbyshire). In the same year, a small farm ('Radford Farm') was established some 300 yards to the west by Richard Radford. He was born in Manchester in *1778, and lived with his wife, Elizabeth, an unmarried daughter and an unmarried son who was described as a 'cow keeper' in the 1851 census.

In 1855 William Prince built another house near his own. This was 'Sale Grove', a pair of semi-detached dwellings. The first occupiers were Edward Higgin, a law clerk, and John Keal (*1820-1890). The latter was a wine merchant with premises at 16, Cupid's Alley, off Deansgate, in Manchester, which he rented from the Atkinson family (see p.31). He was born in Brigg (Lincolnshire) and he and his wife Rebecca had five children and one servant. Within three years both families had moved elsewhere. One of the later residents was Mrs. Mary Baxter, who lived there for sixteen years from 1858. About the same time 'Lyme Grove' was built on the west side of William Prince's house. 'Lyme Grove' consisted of two large houses separated by a short drive; each house was a pair of semi-detached dwellings. The owners were Isaac Storey and Joseph Clarke. Isaac Storey (*1811-79) had moved when the 1861 census was taken, and his son John (*1831-83) was now living in the house; he was a coppersmith and brassfounder, living with his wife, three children, one unmarried brother and one servant. His wife, Eliza, was Joseph Clarke's daughter. The other original occupant was Charles Evans, who also moved away before the 1861 census. Joseph Clarke (*1811-85) was a stationer and printer, born in Manchester. He and his wife Eliza had three children and one servant. The other occupant was Thomas Hawkins, a 'spinner and manufacturer' who was born in Lancashire in *1814.

Later houses on the south side of Marsland Road were 'Beaufort House' (1858) and 'Minerva House' (1860), on George's Road. John Keal and his family moved from 'Sale Grove' to 'Beaufort House' when it was built. The short road upon which it stood took the name 'Beaufort Road', instead of its former more interesting name - 'Boggart Lane'. 'Minerva House' was built for George Cunningham (hence the name of the road). He was a wine and spirit merchant born in Liverpool in *1821. In the 1861 census he was living with three children and his mother-in-law (presumably his wife was away). Before moving to 'Minerva House' the Cunninghams had lived in 'Moss Cottage' on Poplar Grove while their new house was being built. George Cunningham also owned 'Roundland House' on Northenden Road (see p.128). He was accidentally drowned in 1876. One other house was built around 1860 on the south side of Marsland Road, opposite 'Dunham View'. This was the home of Thomas Peers Heywood (*1811-1870). He was born in Manchester and lived with his wife, Edith. They sold beer and spirits, and their premises were known as the 'Brooklands Hotel' until the opening of another hotel with the same name in 1872 (see p.109).

Nearer to Moor Nook, a cottage was built around 1856 on the south side of the road near Moor Nook Farm. This was 'Moorfield Cottage'. The first owner was William Jones, but two years later it was taken by Jacob Bradford (*1820-1867), a toy dealer born in Stockport. He had great ideas for the cottage (see later) and soon bought some of the surrounding area (called 'Boggart Lane Fields').

By 1856 Samuel Brooks owned a substantial part of Sale. Among his purchases were Williamson's Farm and Wright's Farm, bought around 1854. Some six years later he built a road running south-east through the lands of Marsland's farm from the junction of Hope Road and Marsland Road. The new road, originally named 'Brooks's New Road' and later 'Brooks's Drive', ran through Baguley (crossing the Stockport-Altrincham Turnpike near the bridge over the Fairywell Brook) to Hale Barns, where it met the Altrincham-Wilmslow road near 'Prospect House', a total of just over four miles. The date of building the new road is not accurately known. William Wilson's map of Sale (1860) shows the road completed to the township boundary; on the other hand, a milestone in the Baguley section 900 yards beyond the Sale boundary bears the date '1863'. Originally the part of the road between Marsland Road and Altrincham Road (the part now called 'Brooklands Road') had grass verges 25 feet wide on each side of the carriageway, but as each house was built, the owner incorporated the verge into his garden, and over the years the grass verges disappeared completely. The first house built on Brooklands Road was appropriately enough named 'Brooklands House'. This was built for Thomas Kelly, a lace merchant, who moved in with his family in the spring of 1861. Prior to this, they had been living in 'Woodville' on Springfield (off School Road). As they moved to their new house, four other houses were being built on Brooklands Road by Samuel Brooks (see p.109). Thomas was born in Ireland in *1812 and had married a girl from Liverpool.

(iii) Moor Nook

The tenancy of Baxter's Farm at Moor Nook was given to George Brown's younger son, William, in 1843. William (1799-1879) was born in Sale, and lived with his wife, Phoebe. They remained at Moor Mook Farm for 27 years until 1871 (William's elder brother, Peter, rented the Baxter family's other farm in Priory Road).

The two Higson farms were run by James Higson. The larger farm was still leased from Lord Stamford, but the smaller one (the farm originally rented by John Higson junior) was bought in 1847 by John Brogden of 'Priory Gate House'. James Higson still managed the farm but the house was now named 'Raglan House' and was rented out. In 1850 the tenant of the house was a bricklayer from Nottingham, John Morley. He was responsible for building 'Holly Bank' on Derbyshire Road (see p.52). In 1856 he moved into his own house ('Windsor Cottage') and his place at the house was taken by Charles Garner, who was born in Sale in *1831. He looked after the 19-acre farm for John Brogden from around 1856. Three years later John Brogden moved into a new house off Washway Road (see p.102) and transferred the name 'Raglan House' to his own house.

(iv) Marsland Road (east of Derbyshire Road)

Joseph Moore's house on the north side of Marsland Road was enlarged to a terrace of three houses in 1847. The residents were John Ollier (*1808-78), Mrs. Hannah Sutton and Thomas Watson.

Samuel Woodall moved from the Barlow small-holding in 1848, and his place was taken by John Kelsall (*1781-1854). When he died his son Jonathan (1807-1871) succeeded him.

'Brookside' on Washway Road is so named because it stands near the site of Bythell's Bridge (see p.107).

1861-1876

(i) Washway Road

Existing properties

David Bellhouse of 'Sale Heys Cottage' died in 1866; one of his sons, Edward Taylor Bellhouse, then came to live in the house. Edward (1816-1881) was the owner of the Eagle Iron Foundry in Hunt Street, Manchester. His obituary in the 'Manchester Guardian' mentions that his firm installed the lifts in Manchester's new town hall. They had also provided the steelwork for many bridges in the Manchester area, including those on the Manchester, South Junction & Altrincham Railway. In 1851 they had provided a cast-iron ballroom for the Queen at Balmoral Castle. Edward's uncle John lived at 'Beechfield', some 400 yards further down the road. He died in 1863, and his widow, Isabella, stayed on in the house for another six years. 'Beechfield' then became the residence of their son, Walter (*1838-1915). He was a cotton spinner, born in Manchester. He and his family had six servants to look after them.

The other large house in the area, 'Woodheys', was the home of the Critchley family until 1866. From 1870 it was rented by Alexander W. Smith, who was born in Newcastle-upon-Tyne in *1823. He and his family had five servants. He was a director of Arrowsmith & Ryder, wine merchants, at 20, King Street, Manchester. Before coming to Sale, the Smith family had lived in 'Fallowfield Lodge'. John Brogden of 'Raglan House' died in 1869; his widow, Sarah, remained in the house until her death sixteen years later. Joseph Thompson, the owner and builder of 'Raglan House' continued to live next door in 'Hope Cottage' until his death in 1888.

The two farms at the southern end of Washway Road continued to function as normal; they were a long way from the centre of Sale, where most of the new housing was being built. From 1865 New Farm was rented by James Blain (*1828-88), who was born in Weaverham. Washway Farm had several tenants until William Owen took over in 1870. He was born in Timperley in *1837.

New properties

A series of seven houses (mostly semi-detached) was built in 1863-4 at right angles to Washway Road, just over 100 yards south of Marsland Road. Originally named 'Stanley Terrace', they are now part of 'Stanley Mount'. Immediately south of the road leading to them a large semi-detached house was completed in 1864. This was called 'Harboro Villa', taking its name from the road opposite. It is now named 'Brookside', as it is situated next to the old 'Bythell's Bridge', where the Fleam runs under Washway Road. One of the long-term residents was Edwin Simpson (*1825-89), an insurance broker born in Manchester.

In 1866 Joseph Thompson bought a patch of land at the back of 'Raglan House' from the executors of Samuel Brooks; on it he built a large house which he named 'Hiltly'. Access to the house was via a new road named

'Walton Road', which ran from Marsland Road to the end of another new road ('Raglan Road', taking its name from 'Raglan House'). The first tenant was James Miller (1816-1868). He was followed by Robert Marsland, the mill owner, who had been living in 'Beech House', Northenden Road (see p.128). The Marsland family remained in 'Hiltly' for over thirteen years. In 1873 Joseph Thompson sold the house and land back to the executors of Samuel Brooks.

A terrace of three large houses was built in 1872 between Marsland Road and Stanley Mount. Named 'Tatham House', 'Brookfield' and 'Stanley House', they were owned by John Rhodes (1817-95), who lived in 'Stanley House'. A builder born in Yorkshire, he also owned all the houses on Egerton Street.

(ii) Marsland Road west of Derbyshire Road

Existing properties

John Johnson continued to live in Hope Cottage until shortly before his death in 1874. Robert Cookson continued to rent Brooklands Farm until 1865, when he left. From 1867 to 1880 the tenant farmer was Roger Hillkirk, who was born in Tideswell, Derbyshire, in *1815. He was succeeded by his son, William. The Kelly family left 'Brooklands House' after living there for two years. The next residents were John Muir and his family. When John Muir died in 1866, his widow lived there for a further year and then sold the house to Thomas Lloyd, a merchant born in Manchester in *1820. He and his family lived in 'Brooklands House' for over twenty years. The house has been replaced by a block of flats, but the gate-posts are still standing.

Jacob Bradford, the owner of 'Moorfield Cottage', had over the years bought over 10 acres of adjoining land. Here he constructed a series of pleasure gardens containing hot houses, a ballroom (1867) and refreshment rooms. Jacob died in 1867 and his widow Jane took over the venture for the next seven years. She then retired and went to live in St. Ann's Street. In 1878 the hotel (the 'Moorfield Hotel') and the gardens were bought by John Witty (of 'Oaklands House') and managed by his brother (?), Marmaduke. The 'Moorfield Gardens' (also known as 'Sale Botanical Gardens') were immensely popular between 1870 and 1895. By the latter date, the Gardens also contained a band stand, a cycle track, tennis, bowling and boating on an artificial lake. Their position, slightly more than ½-mile from Brooklands Station, meant that there was easy access from all over Manchester. The noise and bustle especially at week-ends did not please some of the more genteel residents in the Marsland Road area. The main building became the 'Sale Hotel' in 1898 and the Gardens were finally sold off in 1902.

The premises of Thomas Peers Heywood were known as the 'Brooklands Hotel' for a number of years until the larger and newer 'Brooklands Hotel' was built at the junction with Hope Road. Thomas Heywood's hotel then became known as 'the Little Brooklands'. Thomas himself died in 1870, and his widow, Edith, continued to run the premises after his death. Williamson's Farm was rented by Richard Hayman until his death in 1863. Several tenant farmers followed him until John Little (1828-1891) took over in 1868. Born in Scotland, he combined the professions of estate agent and farmer.

After being empty for a couple of years Radford Farm was rented in 1865 by Robert Thornhill, who converted the farmhouse into a school for boys, which he named 'Sale High School'. The 1871 census shows that nine pupils were boarders at that time. George Cunningham moved out of 'Minerva House' in 1868 and rented it to the Rev. Thomas Brooke. A new church was consecrated on 9th April, 1868, on Brooklands Road, creating a new parish. The church (dedicated to St. John the Divine) was just over the township boundary, in Baguley, and the Rev. Brooke was the vicar. He was born in Leeds in *1816 and stayed at 'Minerva House' from 1868 until his death in 1875. The four houses of 'Lyme Grove' remained in the ownership of the Clarke and Storey families - in fact, these families continued to own the houses until the 1920's.

New buildings - north side

The opening of the railway station at Marsland's Bridge in 1859 (see p.28) triggered a flurry of house-building on Marsland Road and the neighbouring area. Strangely enough, there was very little development on the north side of Marsland Road itself. In August,1862, a large public cemetery was opened on land west of the canal and railway. The appointed registrar was John Pixton (*1816-1895), who lived in the lodge at the cemetery gates. Previously he and his family had lived in one of the cottages at Moor Nook. As this was one of the first public cemeteries in the Manchester area, the graves contain people from all over Manchester. It was extended in 1876.

In 1867 James Parker bought 1½ acres of land between Wardle Road and Derbyshire Road. Here he built a large house, which he called 'Oaklands'. The house was set back 60 yards from the road, with a large ornamental garden in front of it. James Parker left the house in the summer of 1870 (a year after moving in), and let the house to John Witty, a woollen and linen merchant, born in Manchester in *1831. The house later became part of Sale Girls' Grammar School, which in turn later became Sale Grammar School. In 1873 the new 'Brooklands Hotel' was opened at the junction of Hope Road, near the station. It was owned by Robert Scott, who lived Wardle Road (see p.66). In 1876 it was taken over by the Brooklands Hotel Management Company. Its prime position meant that it soon became extremely popular with businessmen, who only had to walk across the road to catch a train into Manchester. It also was very popular for celebratory dinners and events right up to its closure in 1972.

New buildings - south side

As mentioned earlier, four houses were in the process of being built on Brooklands Road in 1861. These were large detached houses, owned by Samuel Brooks, the banker. The houses were originally all of a similar size and lay-

'Belmore' is the only survivor of the four houses built by Samuel Brooks on Brooklands Road in 1861 (see p.111).

out, although some were subsequently altered and enlarged. Each stood in 3/4 acre of ground. The houses were 'Woodbourne' and 'Fernacre', on the west side of the road, and 'Mersey Lea' and 'Belmore', on the east side. 'Woodbourne' and 'Fernacre' remained empty for nearly two years after completion. In summer 1863 they were both occupied - 'Woodbourne' by Walter Bellhouse, and 'Fernacre' by William Shawcross. Walter Bellhouse was the son of John Bellhouse, who lived at 'Beechfield' on Washway Road. As already mentioned, in 1869 Walter and his family moved to 'Beechfield'. 'Woodbourne' then lay empty for over two years, until it was rented by Christopher Mothersill, a cloth agent, born in Manchester in *1824. He and his family later bought the house and lived in it for twenty years. William Shawcross was a retired merchant, born in Manchester in *1818. He and his family lived in 'Fernacre' for nearly thirty years. 'Mersey Lea' was occupied soon after completion by Henry Brogden (1827-1913), one of the sons of John Brogden. When his father died in 1869, he went to live with his mother in 'Raglan House'. 'Mersey Lea' was then unoccupied for eighteen months. In 1872 Adam Hogg and his family came to live in the house. He was a magistrate and merchant, born in Scotland in *1833. 'Belmore' was the home of William Norris (*1815-70), who gave his name to the short road which ran alongside his house. When he died in 1870 the house lay empty for two years. For two years after that it was occupied by John Slater (*1832-79), then in 1875 it became the home of James Charnock, whose income came from 'land and buildings'. He was born in Cullingworth (near Bradford) in *1840. He changed the name to 'Horton Royde'. The former name 'Belmore' was later restored, and the house (now a hotel) is the only one of the original five houses on Brooklands Road still in existence. Another house was built by the trustees of Samuel Brooks in 1867 further down Brooklands Road. This was 'Ellan Brook'; the house and most of its grounds were in Baguley township, but Baguley Brook ran through the garden, and the small portion to the north of it, including a greenhouse, lay in Sale. The first resident of 'Ellan Brook' was John Kendall, but after two years he moved to a house on Broad Road (see p.90). The next resident was Hermann Zill, a merchant born in Saxony.

A wharf was built on the canal side at Brooklands station, and this was also owned by Samuel Brooks. In 1862 'Brooklands Cottage' and two other houses nearby were completed. 'Brooklands Cottage' was built for George Ellerback (*1799-1881), a retired farmer born in Rochdale. When he died his daughter continued to live in the house. The two semi-detached houses (present numbers 225 and 227, formerly numbers 179 and 181) were the homes of Thomas Buck and Hannah Jones. In 1864 Thomas Heywood built a terrace of four houses next to 'Brooklands Cottage'. They were named 'Brooklands Terrace' and Thomas Heywood's widow went to live in one of the houses when she finally retired from keeping the hotel. One of the houses is now a 'washateria'. These were followed by 'Brooklands Villa', a large house on the corner of Brooklands Crescent, which was just being laid out. 'Brooklands Villa' was

This unusual-looking house, 'Brooklands Cottage', was built in 1862 for George Ellerback (see p.111).

built for John Fereday (*1807-87), an engraver who was born in Birmingham. He and his family lived in the house for twenty-two years. It has now been replaced by a modern building.

Further to the west, John Brogden built a terrace of ten houses, at the end of a short path leading from Marsland Road. These were named 'Brogden Terrace' and were completed early in 1866 (the neighbouring houses in 'Brogden Grove' were not built until 18 years later). About the same time, 'East View' and 'Carlton Villas' and 'Terrace' were completed. 'East View' was on the new loop named Brooklands Crescent. As may be expected, it faced east. For over twenty-five years it was the home of William Brown, a draper born in Manchester in *1818. 'Carlton Villas' and 'Carlton Terrace' consisted of two semi-detached houses ('Carlton Villas') and a row of five terraced houses next to them. They were all owned by Henry Burgess, who lived in one of the semi-detached houses. He was a draper born in Manchester in *1829. The two houses have since been extended, and are now shops (a greengrocer and a confectioner).

Two further developments in the area came a little later. 'Claremont', a large detached house, was built in 1869 on the corner of Brooklands Crescent for Walter Hull, a merchant born in Bedfordshire in *1828. He and his family moved five years later to West Grove. 1873 saw the completion of four shops adjacent to the '(Little) Brooklands Hotel' and a street of houses next to them. The four shops were owned by Robert Scott, and included a butcher, a joiner and a plumber; a slaughterhouse and stables were built behind the shops. For six or seven years the new street next to them was called either 'Marsland Grove' or 'Brooklands Grove', until the name finally became just 'The Grove'.

Completed in late 1871, 'Mitford House' was built on the corner of George's Road and Marsland Road. It consisted of two semi-detached houses, which became the homes of George Gadd and Charles Burchardt (the latter was an analytical chemist born in Prussia). The houses are now a residential home for the elderly.

In 1864 two large houses were completed in Beaufort Road. These were 'Amery Vale' (later number 7) and 'Sandal House' (number 9), the homes for seven years of David W. Brown (*1817-79) and Abraham Crompton. John Keal of 'Beaufort House' built a pair of large semi-detached houses between his own house and Marsland Road in 1872. The tenants of these houses (numbers 1 and 3) were John Campbell, a packing-case manufacturer born in Salford in *1820, and Thomas Warburton, about whom we have no information. Three years later John Keal and his family moved to a new house ('Brookfield') on Northenden Road. At the same time, D.W. Brown moved into a smaller house while retaining ownership of 'Amery Vale'. His new house was probably the first on what later became 'Beaufort Avenue'.

(iii) Moor Nook

Moor Nook Farm continued to be run by William Brown until his retirement in 1871. It was then rented by James Simpson. The other farm at Moor Nook, Brogden's Farm, was tenanted by Charles Garner until 1868, when John Gough took over. The latter was born in Sale in *1823 and had lived in one of the cottages at Moor Nook for many years. He had probably worked on Brogden's Farm before he became the tenant farmer. In 1873 the farm was sold by Mrs. Brogden to Joseph Clarke, who lived in 'Lyme Grove'.

(iv) Marsland Road east of Derbyshire Road

Three separate terraces of cottages were built between 1861 and 1876. First were the six cottages called 'Hill End View'. These built in 1864 and were were owned by John Bellis. They were later numbered 16 to 26 Marsland Road. They were followed by a further six cottages built three years later, and owned by John Hampson. These became numbers 4 to 14. Most of these cottages were demolished to make way fro a one-way road system; three only remain. Lastly, a terrace of eleven houses was built in 1870 on a new street running at right-angles to Marsland Road, between the old Barlow Farm and the 'Legh Arms'. When completed there were thirty-two houses ('St. Margaret's View'); the street ('Perseverance Street') finally became part of Conway Road.

The small 5-acre 'farm' which had been the Barlow Farm was now a market garden, managed by Jonathan Kelsall until 1869. It was then rented by William Baldwin. He was born in Sale in *1846 and later moved to Moor Nook Farm, which he ran for many years. Three houses were built in 1875 near to the farm They were owned by William Hartley, who lived in one of them. He was a bricklayer born in Sale in *1815. Originally 15-19 Marsland Road, they are now numbered 23-27.

8. THE DEVELOPMENT OF EASTERN SALE 1806-1876

The area covered by this chapter is the whole of Sale east of an imaginary line drawn south from the River Mersey, down Old Hall Road to the 'Legh Arms' and then south to Baguley Brook. It includes Sale Old Hall and Wallbank Farm in the north, and Lime Tree Farm in the south. It also includes Sale New Hall and Sale Green, the centre of mediaeval Sale (see map p.30).

In 1806 the area was one of scattered farms and fields enclosed by hedges. The roads which existed then were Old Hall Road, Baguley Road, Northenden Road, Wythenshawe Road, Rutland Lane and Fairy Lane. All these followed their present-day course with the exceptions of three roads which were altered when the M63 motorway was built through Sale in 1973-4 - these were Old Hall Road, Rutland Lane and Fairy Lane. A small section of the original road to the Old Hall can be seen at the junction of Dane Road and Old Hall Road, running behind the Dovecoat Centre. The triangle at the junction of Old Hall Road and Northenden Road was waste land, as was an area to the east of Baguley Road at this point.

The Area in 1806
(i) From the River Mersey to Sale Green

Sale Old Hall stood near the northern end of Old Hall Road. Here the road divided into two tracks, one leading northwards to Jackson's Ford over the Mersey and the other running north-east to Jackson's Ferry. The Hall was built by the Massey family around 1600 AD probably on the site of an earlier manor house. The exact shape of the Hall in 1806 is not clear; the Pre-Enclosure Map shows it as a rectangular building, whereas the Legh Estate Map of 1801 shows it as having two small wings. A farm of 62 acres was attached to the Hall, the fields extending to the River Mersey. In 1806 the Hall was rented from George J. Legh and Wilbraham Egerton by Thomas Mort, a merchant who also had a house in King Street, Manchester. Alice Norris (some relation?) also lived in the Hall, and she ran the farm. She was the widow of Samuel Norris, who rented the Hall from some time before 1780 to his death in 1791 (see p.148).

Wallbank Farm stood to the west of the Hall. It belonged to Dr. Charles White and in 1806 had been rented for over twenty-five years by William Alderley (*1745-1812). At nearly 53 acres it was one of the largest farms in Sale. On the same side of the road and nearer to Dane Road were the cottage and garden which James Brownhill rented from Elizabeth Whitwell. There were two cottages at the junction with Dane Road. These belonged to Joseph Warburton, and were the homes of John Cookson and Edward Hampson (see p.74).

The area round the junctions of Dane Road and Broad Road with Old Hall

115

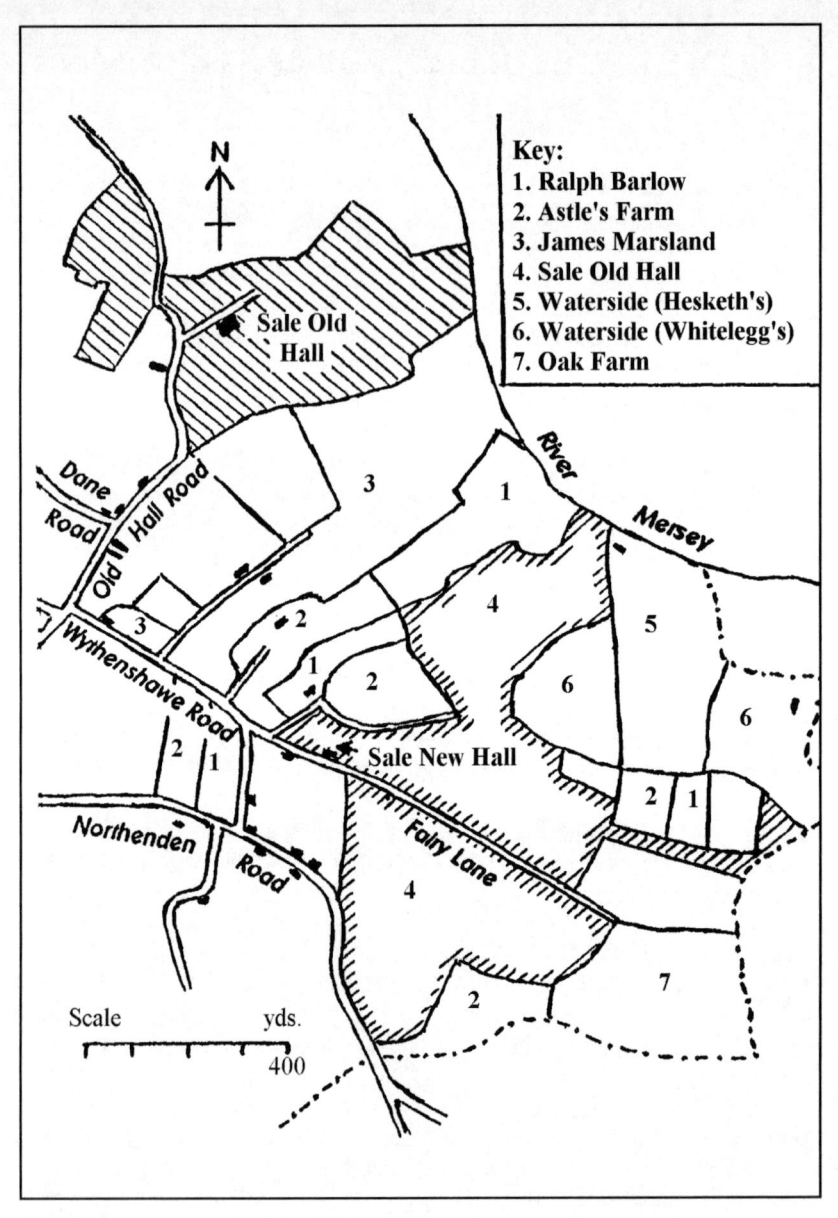

Farms in eastern Sale in 1806

Road was 'Sale Green'. A small cottage stood opposite the end of Dane Road; this was the home of William Gough (*1752-1825) and next to it was a row of 5 cottages ('Sale Green Cottages') belonging to John Higson, who farmed at Moor Nook.

(ii) Sale Green to the 'Legh Arms'

It is probable that the road leading from the 'Legh Arms' to the Old Hall did not have a separate name in 1806, but we do know that the crossroads at the junction of Broad Road, Old Hall Road and Wythenshawe Road was known as 'Four Lane Ends'. The only property on Old Hall Road between Broad Road and Northenden Road was 'Sale Cottage', a largish house standing in its own grounds. It was situated opposite the end of Baguley Road, and was owned by John Cookson (*1749-1819), who had lived in it for over twenty years. The site is now occupied by a block of flats named 'Old Hall Court'.

(iii) Wythenshawe Road, Rutland Lane and Fairy Lane

The name 'Wythenshawe Road' was not used until 1867, when many of Sale's roads were re-named. Before this date its name seem to be undecided (see the examples quoted on p.17). A few yards along Wythenshawe Road from Four Lane Ends was the house belonging to James Marsland (*1767-1824). He owned a farm (39 acres) and also a row of cottages (see below). In addition he rented a farm from Ralph Ashton at the junction of Old Hall Road and Dane Road.

100 yards along Wythenshawe Road from Four Lane Ends, Rutland Lane runs off to the left. In 1806 it was called 'Davenport Lane', because it led to cottages and fields belonging to the Davenport family. These were on the left hand side of the lane and the occupier in 1806 was George Davenport. Further up Rutland Lane, on the other side, was a row of cottages inhabited by various tenants; their landlord was James Marsland. The next short track off Wythenshawe Road led to Astle's Farm. One of the buildings was the home of Miss Mary Astle ('Astley' in the earlier Land Tax Returns); she also had two large fields. The rest of the farm was rented from her by Robert Marsland and others. The total area of the farm was 31 acres.

Fairy Lane ran off to the east at the point where Wythenshawe Road turned south. At the junction was a large pond, probably the remains of an old marl pit. A short road on the left hand side of Fairy Lane led to a 24-acre farm rented by Ralph Barlow (junior) from Lord Stamford. This later became known as 'Gratrix's Farm' (see below). Further along there were two properties, one on each side of the road. On the left were the buildings of Sale New Hall; it has usually been accepted that it was built in 1688 by William, the younger son of James Massey, but there is evidence that it existed some thirty years earlier. It was now the centre of a large farm (77 acres) owned by Dr. Charles White. The tenant farmer was William Cookson (*1767-1827). James Hunt (*1764-1835) had a house and smallholding opposite the New Hall.

Fairy Lane also led to three other farms. The one nearest to the Mersey was called appropriately enough 'Waterside'. It was owned by Thomas Hesketh and farmed by Edward Gratrix. Further east, almost on the township boundary were Waterside Farm and Oak Farm. Waterside Farm (24 acres) was owned by William Whitelegg of Northenden, and farmed by John Alderley. Oak Farm seems to have been in 1806 merely part of another farm based in Northenden, as there was no farmhouse on the Sale side of the boundary until a later date. Its 9 fields (18 acres) were owned and farmed by John Schofield (also spelt 'Scholefield').

There were two cottages on the section of Wythenshawe Road between Fairy Lane and Northenden Road. The first was the home of David Parnell (or 'Parnil') (*1744-1818) and the second was the home of John Marsland (*1764-1807, the brother of James above). The latter's house still stands at the junction of Wythenshawe Road and Northenden Road. Opposite the house was a guidepost which was often referred to in contemporary documents.

(iv) Northenden Road from the 'Legh Arms' to the boundary

Until 1867 Northenden Road was called 'Moor Lane' from the bridge over the canal to the guidepost at the junction with Wythenshawe Road. From here to the township boundary it was 'Hart Lane'.

North side

After Baguley Lane there were two properties on the north side before the junction with Wythenshawe Road. The first was a 5-acre smallholding owned and run by Lucy, the widow of William Dewsbury; this later became 'Victoria Farm'. The second was 'Yew Tree Cottage', a house and garden occupied by Edward Marsland. It still stands on Northenden Road.

South side

The 'Legh Arms' at the junction of Northenden Road and Marsland Road was listed in 1806 as a 'building & garden' and seems to have been a smithy. Owned by G.J. Legh, it was the home of Robert Marsland (d.1806), who lived with his wife Sarah and had a smallholding (5 acres) behind the building. The next property, at the corner of Baguley Lane, was Roylance's Farm. This was a 15-acre farm which for twenty-five years had been rented from G.J. Legh by William Roylance (*1737-1819). He lived with his wife Martha. Further on there were four houses. The first three were occupied by Ann Brownhill, Hugh Gresty, and Betty Renshaw; the fourth, at the end of Gratrix Lane, was set back from the road and was in fact two cottages, the homes of Edmund Royle and Esther Hurlbutt, a widow. At the top of Gratrix Lane Peter Gratrix lived in a house which later became the 'Lindow Tavern'. Even in 1806 the building was called the 'Lindow Building' and it is probable that Peter Gratrix sold beer.

Further towards Northenden, past John Marsland's house at the corner of Wythenshawe Road, there were two houses on the left hand side of

'Yew Tree Cottage' on Northenden Road dates back to the eighteenth century (see p.118).

Northenden Road and one on the right. Those on the left were the homes of John Newton and Ralph Barlow (senior); the one on the right was owned and occupied by Timothy Leigh (d.1811) and his wife Martha. He also owned 15 acres behind the house, which were rented from him and farmed by William Cookson of Sale New Hall.

(v) South of Northenden Road

325 yards down Baguley Lane stood the buildings of Lime Tree Farm. With an area of 119 acres it was the second largest farm in Sale. It was owned by Wilbraham Egerton of Tatton and for over 25 years had been rented by Jonathan Renshaw (*1754-1833) with his wife Hannah. Further down the road became a mere footpath, leading to a footbridge across Baguley Brook. Before the bridge was reached a track led off to the buildings of Chadwick's Farm ('Beech Farm'). The thirteen fields covered 67 acres, stretching in a long, thin shape sometimes only one field deep, near to and partly next to Baguley Brook. The farm took its name from the tenant farmer John Chadwick (*1749 -1818) who rented the farm from Dr. White. 525 yards to the east a track followed the present line of Gratrix Lane and Sandbach Road, and in the bend of the latter stood the farm buildings of the 35-acre farm belonging to Edward Gratrix. His fields ran down to the township boundary (see map on p.116). Edward also owned the 'Lindow Building' (see above).

1806-1841

The story of the area between 1806 and 1841 is mostly a series of changes of ownership of buildings and farms. Few new houses were built during the period.

(i) From the River Mersey to Sale Green

Soon after 1806 George Legh sold Sale Old Hall to John Moore and his son John. The date is usually quoted as 1817, but the Land Tax Returns show John Moore and his son as the owners in 1807. John Moore senior also bought the title of 'Lord of the Manor' in 1810. The Hall continued to be let until 1822 (see p.148). It seems to have been a school from 1818 to 1821, when a Mr. Bury rented it. In 1822 one of the Moores possibly took up residence (the name then appears as the occupant until 1839). John Moore senior died in 1826 and fourteen years later his son, who had now moved to Cornbrook Terrace, Stretford, sold the Hall to Mrs. Mary Worthington (*1778-1854) of Altrincham. She was the widow of Hugh Worthington, attorney and legal adviser to Lord Stamford. Her husband had died in 1839, and it then seemed reasonable to move with her son, Robert, nearer to the latter's practice in Manchester. Mrs Worthington was well acquainted with Sale, as her father, the Rev. Robert Harrop, of Hale Barns, had been minister of Cross Street chapel in Sale for many years. She had the Hall rebuilt before taking up residence there. The Worthingtons were now Lords of the Manor.

When William Alderley died in 1812 the tenancy of Wallbank Farm went to his third son, Samuel (*1788-1867). By purchasing land himself and renting fields from other owners he doubled the area of the farm to 108 acres. Samuel's two older brothers, Thomas and William, lived elsewhere in Sale.

The Enclosure maps are not clear as to whether there were two rows of cottages at Sale Green in 1806 (there is a fold in the map at a critical point). Certainly by 1836 there was a second row, owned by Ellen Cheetham.

Edmund Howarth (1764-1855) was a merchant born in Blackburn; he had married Elizabeth Peel, a cousin of Sir Robert Peel (Prime Minister from 1841 to 1846). When his wife died, Edmund decided to move to Sale. In 1831 he bought a plot of land, part of the Sale Old Hall estate. Five years later he owned 42 acres, on which stood his new house, 'Sale Lodge' (now the club house of Sale Golf Club). He then continued to enlarge his estate by buying the surrounding land over the following fifteen years (see p.126).

(ii) Sale Green to the 'Legh Arms'

From 1818 'Sale Cottage' on Old Hall Road was rented by various gentlemen until around 1833, when Richard Leigh Trafford (1800-1864) moved in with his wife, Eliza. They had five children and six servants. Richard was a barrister with premises at 3, St. James's Square, Manchester. He bought the property six years after moving in.

(iii) Wythenshawe Road, Rutland Lane and Fairy Lane

As mentioned on page 21, Thomas Hesketh's farm disappeared in 1807, the land being divided between Sale New Hall Farm and Waterside Farm. The farm buildings ('Waterside Cottages') continued to be occupied by farm labourers. Waterside Farm was rented by John Alderley until 1827. There were then a number of tenants over the following years and from 1836 to 1842 the tenant farmer was Peter Gratrix, junior. Oak Farm continued under John Schofield ('Scholefield') until 1830, when it was then divided between John Strettell and John Gresty. They continued to farm there for ten years. Early in 1841 both parts were bought by Samuel Lyth, and it is as 'Lyth's Farm' that the farm was known for the next forty years.

James Marsland died in 1824 and his farm was first run by his widow, Betty, and then by his eldest son, John (1796-1877). By the time of the 1841 census John had moved to a farm on Woodhouse Lane (Ashton-on-Mersey), owned by William Wainman. Later he took up the tenancy of Chapel Lane Farm; at the same time he still retained ownership of 37 acres, mostly those fields which had been allocated to the family at the Enclosure of 1807. These were over a mile away, on both sides of Marsland Road. The cottages ('Marsland Houses') on the east side of Rutland Lane were the homes of various families, and James Marsland's widow, Betty, was living with her younger son, James (b. *1805), in 'Howarth's Houses' on the west side of Rutland Lane. The house near the junction of Wythenshawe Road and Old Hall Road was now the home of Edward Gresty. James junior was still running the family farm at Rutland Lane, but it had now been sold with the cottages to Edmund Howarth.

Astle's Farm continued to be split into several parts. The main part near the house was rented by Thomas Chadwick from 1820 to 1843 and later by William Cuff; two large fields to the east were rented by John Gresty, and later by Joseph Morgan (see below). Ralph Barlow's farm was sold in 1828 to George Gratrix, and from that date was referred to as 'Gratrix's Farm'. In 1840 the tenancy was taken by Joseph Morgan, who moved to Sale from a farm in Timperley. Joseph (*1800-1868) was born in Lymm and in 1851 was living with his wife, Frances, and eight children. As already mentioned, he also farmed part of the neighbouring Astle's Farm. The family ran these farms for nearly forty years.

In 1821 William Cookson handed over the tenancy of Sale New Hall to his son, also named William. He in turn was succeeded by Samuel Faulkner in 1826. The latter died two years later and the farm was run by his widow, Martha, for the next three years. The farm was then run by another widow, Sarah Whitelegg (*1764-1844).

A new house was built around 1834 on Wythenshawe Road, just south of the junction with Fairy Lane. This was 'Poole Croft' and was the home of Samuel Moxon (*1779-1866), who rented it with 6 acres of ground from John Harrison. Samuel was a farmer born in London. In 1841 a new cottage was built at the junction of Wythenshawe Road and Old Hall Road. This was the home of John Alderley, a shopkeeper born in *1807 at Dunham Massey. John Marsland's house at the junction of Wythenshawe Road and Northenden Road was now a shop, run by Mary Sutherland.

(iv) Northenden Road from the 'Legh Arms' to the boundary

George Oldfield moved from the bottom of School Road to Robert Marsland's smithy in 1812. He lived there with his second wife, Sarah, until he died in 1823. He probably sold beer in addition to plying his trade, and as Sarah continued to live there for another ten years or so, she probably carried on the sale of beer. By 1836 it had been taken over by Thomas Brickell (*1802-67), a wheelwright born in Northenden. He lived with his wife, Mary. Later the property became the 'Legh Arms' (see p.127).

When William Roylance died in 1819, the tenancy of the farm was taken by Thomas Renshaw (*1793-1866). Nine years later he moved to Whitehall Farm, and Roylance's Farm was taken over by John Cordingley, a farmer from Northenden who had married a Sale girl. John was the brother of Joseph at Miry Gate Farm.

In 1821 William Cookson senior (*1767-1827) moved from Sale New Hall to Timothy Leigh's house and farm on Hart Lane. When he died his widow Mary (*1773-1856) continued to live there for a number of years (see below).

In 1839 the Primitive Methodists opened their first chapel in Sale, on the north side of Northenden Road between 'Yew Tree Cottage' and the guide post. It was rebuilt in 1873, and is still in use for worship.

At sometime between 1831 and 1836 the 'Barracks' were built opposite Roylance's Farm. Although this was intended to be purely temporary housing, it was still there in 1876. About the same time two cottages were built nearer to Baguley Road. One of these was the home of John Tyrer (*1773-1847), a retired butcher. The cottages were later extended to form 'Roundland Terrace'.

By 1841 John Holland (*1774-1843) had established a small farm around what had been Betty Renshaw's house. The Renshaw family had moved to a new house and market garden reached down a lane running by the side of John Holland's house. The two fields were purchased from the Sale Old Hall estate in 1824 by James Renshaw (*1763-1829). Another small farm or market garden had been established at the bottom of Gratrix Lane. This was 'Holly Hey', occupied by James Woodall junior (b.*1804), who had bought a 5-acre field from the Sale Old Hall estate around 1835. He lived with his wife, Charlotte, and their young family.

The cottages on the south side of Northenden Road had a number of residents during the period 1806-41. Elizabeth Whitwell's cottage was now the home of John Whitehead; Hugh Gresty's cottage had become the property of the Woodall family in 1825. In 1841 it was occupied by Thomas Marsland (*1799-1870). The cottages of Esther Hurlbutt and Edmund Royle had become a farmhouse, occupied by three families of agricultural workers. Young Edward Gratrix and his wife were at the 'Lindow'. In 1841 he was described as a farmer, but ten years later he was a 'beer-seller'.

The rows of cottages on both sides of Northenden Road between Wythenshawe Road and the township boundary were extended. One of the inhabitants was now a beer-seller named Obadiah Leigh (*1807-1856). In addition to the cottages two large houses were built on the south side; Mary, the widow of William Cookson senior, moved into one ('Beech House'); the other ('Boundary House', built in 1838) was the home of Paul Marple, a widower and 'proprietor of houses'. He was born in Staveley (Derbyshire) in *1777 and died in Sale in 1858.

(v) South of Northenden Road

In 1807 Wilbraham Egerton and G.C. Legh sold Lime Tree Farm to Matthew Shawcross. Two years later it was sold again, 51 acres going to the Rev. Robert Harrop of Hale and 20 acres to Charles White. For most of the nineteenth century the remaining 46 acres were known as 'Shawcross's Farm'. Until 1825 it was farmed by Peter Gratrix and from 1826 the tenant farmer was William Dewsbury. Charles White sold Chadwick's Farm in 1809 to the Rev. Harrop. In 1827 both of the Rev. Harrop's plots were bought by Francis Woodiwiss, and from this date the combined Beech Farm was usually known as 'Woodiwiss's Farm', although it was still run by the same two tenant farmers. John Hampson (*1789-1879) was born in Stretford, and he lived with his wife, Sarah. They stayed at Beech Farm for over fifty years.

Edward Gratrix's farm on Sandbach Road continued to be run by successive members of the family. In 1841 the farm was run by John Gratrix, who was aged 33. Old Peter Gratrix (his father) lived with him.

1841-1861

A detailed picture of the area and its inhabitants in 1841 is given in *Sale, Cheshire, in 1841*, pages 66-68 and 71-76.

As this area of Sale lay furthest from the railway, the impact of the latter was minimal, and there was very little change during the period 1841 to 1861. A small number of new houses were built but the area remained overwhelmingly agricultural.

(i) From the River Mersey to Sale Green

The Worthington family temporarily left Sale Old Hall in 1847. Robert Worthington moved to Crumpsall Hall in Manchester, and his mother Mary went to live with her younger son, James, in Sandiway Road, Altrincham. For sixteen years Sale Old Hall was let out to various professional men until James (1817-1887) returned to take up residence in 1863 (see p.148). The three men who rented the Hall in turn during this period were Edward Lyon, John Peel, and Matthew Curtis. The last-named was born in Manchester in 1808. He described himself as a 'machinist' on the 1861 census, whereas in fact he employed 1500 men in a factory making various machines. He was Mayor of Manchester three times, the first occasion being 1860-1 when he lived in Sale Old Hall.

Wallbank Farm continued to be run by Samuel Alderley until around 1854, when he handed it over to his son, Jabez. Samuel then moved to 'Allington Cottages', a pair of semi-detached houses just completed between the corner of Dane Road and Hannah Clarke's house. Samuel later moved to Wallbank Terrace (see below) where he died in 1867.

When Edmund Howarth died in 1855, his son, also named Edmund, was also living in 'Sale Lodge', but he soon moved elsewhere (he owned other properties in Derbyshire). From 1859 the house was let to William Henry Bradley, a manufacturer, who moved from Bury New Road (Manchester) with his family.

In 1858 a terrace of three houses ('Massey Place') was built between Sale Green Cottages and Four lane Ends. The inhabitants in 1861 were Thomas Crowther (a carpenter), Peter Frier (a gardener), and William Pearson (a coachman and domestic servant).

(ii) Sale Green to the 'Legh Arms'

'Sale Cottage' was sold by Richard Leigh Trafford to William Tebbutt in 1846. The latter was a grocer with premises at 4, Victoria Street, and 19, Market Place, Manchester. Born in Lincolnshire in *1810, he lived in 'Sale Cottage' with his wife, Esther, three children and four servants for nine years until 1855, when they all moved out. The new occupier was James Kennedy, a member of the Manchester Stock Exchange. Born in Manchester in *1808, he lived with his wife, Fanny, and two servants. William Tebbutt continued to own the house until his death in 1862, and Old Hall Road was known as 'Tebbutt's Lane' for twenty years up to 1867.

Two pairs of semi-detached houses were built on Old Hall Road in 1855. The owner was Samuel Alderley, who named them 'Wallbank Terrace' after the farm he had rented for many years. Four years later another pair of semi-detached houses was built to the south of them. These were named 'Birchfield' and were also owned by Samuel Alderley. The inhabitants of the six houses in 1861 were Robert Moore (an agent for oils and tallow, born in Manchester in *1835), Peter Potts (a baker, born in Macclesfield in *1817), John Wright (a potato dealer, born in Cheadle in *1830), Hamlett Barlow (a gardener, born in Manchester in *1833), and James Hampson (a land surveyor, born in Sale in *1842). One house was unoccupied at the time. The four houses of Wallbank Terrace (58 to 64 Old Hall Road) are still lived in today, but 'Birchfield' has been demolished.

(iii) Wythenshawe Road, Rutland Lane & Fairy Lane

Rutland Lane was called 'Howarth's Lane' in the 1861 census.

In 1843 Sarah Whitelegg handed over the tenancy of Sale New Hall Farm to Thomas Barlow, who had hitherto been at Temple Farm. She died soon afterwards at the age of 79. Thomas Barlow remained at the farm until his death in 1852. The tenancy was then given first to Thomas Pearson, then to Thomas Leigh, who farmed here for nine years.

In 1841 Thomas Chadwick retired from Astle's Farm and went to live in the cottage which had formerly belonged to David Parnell, on Wythenshawe Road. James Brookes (1812-1892) moved into Samuel Moxon's house ('Poole Croft') in 1848. Born in Sale, he farmed the six acres owned by John Harrison. His wife, Mary, was probably Samuel Moxon's daughter. Samuel had retired but still lived in the house.

By 1854 Edmund Howarth had purchased most of the lands belonging to the old Marsland Farm, some of the Old Hall Estate, the rows of cottages on Rutland Lane, and also the residential part of Astle's Farm upon Mary Astle's death. The latter now became a large house ('The Oaks') surrounded by a market garden. It was rented by James Hodgson (*1808-1867). He was a 'landed proprietor', born in Lancashire. He lived with his wife, Lucy Ann, two sons and two servants. In 1854 Edmund Haworth also had a school built for children who lived on the eastern side of Sale. Called 'Sale Lodge School', it was not at Sale Lodge itself; the school was at the junction of Wythenshawe Road and Fairy Lane. The schoolmistress was Anne Baker.

By 1855 John Marsland's old house on Wythenshawe Road had been rebuilt and converted into a pair of large semi-detached houses. This was 'Mayfield'; one of the houses was the home of Horatio Davenport, the owner. He was a goods buyer for export, born in Manchester in *1808. A bachelor for many years, he lived with two servants. The occupier of the other half was John Medcalf (*1823-88), a merchant born in Manchester. He lived with his wife,

Elizabeth, six children and three servants.

Several other houses were built in the vicinity in 1857. John Alderley's house at the corner of Old Hall Road and Wythenshawe Road was enlarged into a pair of semi-detached houses and another pair of semis (numbers 5 and 7) were built between them and 'Mayfield'. One of the inhabitants was John Farrell, a salesman who lived with his family in number 3 for twenty years. 'Mayfield' has been demolished, but the houses numbered 3,5 and 7 have survived.

Two pairs of semi-detached houses were built on the south side, opposite 'Mayfield'. The first pair ('Fernbank' and 'Meadow View' (later 'Hope Villa')) were the homes of James Hooton and William Smith. James was a salesman born in Dukinfield in 1829. He and his family remained in the house until his death in 1894. William Smith was a merchant born in Sandbach in *1825. The second pair of houses were approached by a track leading from the road. These were a market-garden and nursery belonging to Thomas Kelsall and John Brownhill.

Waterside Farm was tenanted by James Carter from 1843 to 1848 and then by Samuel Woodall (1808-1893). The neighbouring farm ('Lyth's') was rented by Thomas Smith from 1844. Thomas (1820-1906) was the son of William Smith of Clark's Hey. He was born in Sale and lived with his wife, Hannah.

The shop at the corner of Wythenshawe Road and Northenden Road had become a public-house by 1859. Called the 'Nag's Head', it was run by James Sutherland (*1833-90), who was born in Hale. The 'Nag's Head' continued to sell beer and spirits right into the twentieth century.

(iv) Northenden Road from the 'Legh Arms' to the boundary

Sarah, the wife of John Cordingley at Roylance's Farm, died in 1841 and four years later he moved back to Northenden with his two daughters. From 1850 the farm was tenanted by John Heywood (junior)(*1807-1869). John was born in Manchester, and lived with his wife, Jane, and three sons. In 1847 the farm was bought by Samuel Brooks.

In 1842 the beer-shop at the junction of Northenden Road and Marsland Road became the 'Legh Arms' and five years later it was sold by G.C. Legh to Samuel Brooks. The financial success of Thomas Brickell as a publican may be judged from the fact that by the time he retired in 1860 he owned 'Oak Bank' (a row of four houses in Temple Road), two houses in Oak Road and six cottages at Sale Green. When he left the 'Legh Arms' he went to live with his wife in 'Oak Bank'.

By 1849 the terraces of cottages on each side of Northenden Road east of the 'Guidepost' had been enlarged again. There were now seven cottages (owned by Robert Meadowcroft) on the north side and eight (owned by Thomas Cookson) on the south side. Obediah Leigh moved across the road and started to sell his beer from one of the cottages. It later became the 'Jolly

Carter' (now the 'Carter's Arms'). When he died his wife Dinah (*1805-80) continued the trade. The 'Lindow Tavern' was now run by Sarah Gratrix, the daughter-in-law of Edward. She was born in Stretford in *1799.

In 1846 Mary Cookson moved out of 'Beech House' into one of the cottages owned by her family. 'Beech House' was then enlarged and rented by Robert Marsland, the owner of a cotton spinning mill in Ancoats. He was born in Timperley in *1813 and lived with his wife Sarah, two daughters and two servants. Around the same time a pair of semi-detached houses were built between 'Beech House' and 'Boundary House'. These were the homes of Jonathan Gresty and John Brickell. The latter was a bachelor living with his brother Thomas and sister Sarah, both of whom were also unmarried. The houses are still lived in today.

A detached house was built in 1856 at the junction of Baguley Road and Northenden Road. This was 'Roundland House', owned by George Cunningham (see p.104). At first it was rented by John King (*1820-1875), a manufacturer. In 1860 he and his family moved to Holly Bank; 'Roundland House' was then rented by Michael Potter (*1809-1875/6). He was a partner in the firm of Potter & Knight, solicitors, of Manchester. Born in Prestwich, he lived with his wife, Ann, and two servants. About the same time as 'Roundland House' was built, a pair of semi-detached houses were completed near the Barracks. These were named 'Roundland Cottage', and one of residents for many years was James Aldcroft, a blacksmith born in Baguley in *1807. The houses are still lived in today.

A terrace of ten houses was built in 1854-5 on the north side of Northenden Road, just west of the junction with Wythenshawe Road. These were at right angles to the road, and were named 'Moorfield Place'. The inhabitants were mostly agricultural labourers and cleaning ladies.

After Paul Marples' death 'Boundary House' had a series of owners and residents.

'Yew Tree Cottage' had a new owner in 1858, when William Hickman bought the house from James Barrow. William was retired, born in Shropshire in *1804.

(v) South of Northenden Road

The various farms in the east and south of this area of Sale continued to run as before, with several changes of tenancy and ownership. When William Dewsbury retired from Shawcross's (Lime Tree) Farm in 1850 he was followed by John Smith, who managed the farm until 1868. John was born in Heaton Norris (near Stockport) in *1818 and lived with his wife, Elizabeth. Woodiwiss's (Beech) Farm continued to be run by John Hampson until after 1876 and by Edward Gresty until around 1852.

James Woodall retired from Holly Hey in 1859 and rented it to John Kelsall, who was born in Stretford in *1818. Soon after taking over Holly Hey, John Kelsall bought most of the Gratrix Farm next door.

William Bardsley ran the Renshaw Farm from 1849. He was born in Sale in *1808.

1861-1876
(i) The River Mersey to Sale Green

The Worthington family moved back into Sale Old Hall in the summer of 1863. The new resident was James (1817-1887), the second surviving son of Hugo and Mary Worthington. He was born in Altrincham and had spent some years in Shanghai as an East India merchant. When he returned to England he married Mary, the eldest daughter of Henry McConnell, who owned one of largest mills in Manchester. He bought back much of the land which Edmund Howarth had purchased some twenty or thirty years earlier (see below). He was also a Justice of the Peace. The Worthingtons had eight servants to run the Hall.

'Sale Lodge' was one of the properties bought by James Worthington from Edmund Howarth's son. The Bradley family continued to live in it until 1865; it was then rented by John Stott Milne, a collier born in Rochdale in *1827. He remained at 'Sale Lodge' for twenty years. Jabez Alderley left Wallbank Farm when his father died in 1867. The new tenant was John Wood (1828-1908), who also took over New Hall Farm in the following year. He was born in Flixton, and lived with his wife, Ann, and six step-children.. The two farms together were by far the largest unit in Sale - over 200 acres (roughly 10% of the whole of Sale). The 1871 census reveals that John Wood lived at Wallbank Farm rather than in the New Hall. In addition to managing the two largest farms in Sale, he later took over a grocer's and provision shop at the corner of Marsland Road and Northenden Road. He also owned five other shops on Northenden Road and six houses in Sale.

(ii) Sale Green to the 'Legh Arms'

Samuel Alderley moved from 'Allington Cottage' to 'Wallbank Terrace' when his second wife, Sarah, died in 1862. 'Allington Cottage' was then sold to Samuel Brooks, who rented it to Charles W. Wright (1820-1902), a calico merchant born in Nottinghamshire.

It seems that William Tebbut returned to 'Sale Cottage' in 1861, but the rate books are unclear on the matter. He died in 1862, and two years later the Cottage was bought from his executors by John Duncan (1817-93), a baker born in Gainsborough. He remained at 'Sale Cottage' for thirteen years before moving to Alexandra Road. It seems likely that he was one of the founders of 'Duncan and Foster' the Manchester firm of confectioners.

During the period 1861-1871 a number of new houses were built on Old Hall Road. These consisted of numbers 101-103 (a pair of semi-detached houses built opposite 'Wallbank Terrace'), numbers 19-21 (a pair of semi-detached houses built in 1868, now nos. 21 and 23), and two terraces of four houses, one on each side of the road near the junction with Northenden Road. Numbers 101 and 103 were quite substantial and bore names ('Bank View' and 'Pengwyn House'). They were built in 1863 and were the homes of

Samuel Street (*1834-1919, a buyer, born in Manchester) and James Hall (a solicitor's clerk, born in Cheshire in *1831). The houses have been replaced by a block of flats ('Worthington Court'). The terrace of houses built opposite the 'Legh Arms' was a row of shops. They were the homes of David Frith (a draper and provision dealer), Philip Howitt (a joiner born in Nottinghamshire in *1838, probably the son of John Howitt of Derbyshire Road), James Lamb (a brick and tile dealer) and Thomas Knowles (a toolmaker).

In 1867 a terrace of four houses was built on the west side of Baguley Road. These were named 'Peace Terrace'.

(iii) Wythenshawe Road, Rutland Lane and Fairy Lane

The physical appearance of this part of Sale remained virtually unchanged during the years 1861 to 1876, as only one new house was built. The only changes were in the ownership and tenancy of existing properties. As already mentioned, when James Worthington moved back into Sale Old Hall he bought back many of properties and much of the land which his mother had sold to Edmund Howarth. He became the owner of 'Sale Lodge', 'The Oaks', Old Hall Farm, the western half of Astle's Farm, and the cottages on Rutland Lane. The two farms were still run by James Marsland. 'The Oaks' was the home of James Hodgson until his death in 1867; his widow then lived there for another four years. In 1872 it became the home of Michael Potter, who had lived in Roundland House some five years earlier.

Sale Lodge School continued as a school until 1906. For many years the eastern half of Astle's Farm had been farmed by the tenant of Gratrix's Farm next door, and for 28 years the two farms were managed by Joseph Morgan. When he died in 1868 one of his six sons, James, took over. Thomas Leigh continued to rent New Hall Farm until 1867, when his place was taken by John Wood, who also ran Wallbank Farm (see p.130). Samuel Woodall remained tenant of Waterside Farm until 1869. The farm was then run by Thomas Smith, who already managed the neighbouring Lyth's Farm.

The only new property was a pair of large semi-detached houses built on the corner of Wythenshawe Road and Rutland Lane in 1863. As they were owned by Horatio Davenport, they were at first regarded as part of 'Mayfield', although they were 100 yards away from the original 'Mayfield'. The houses later became numbers 29 and 31 Wythenshawe Road, and eventually had their own names. Horatio Davenport himself moved away from 'Mayfield' for a few years from 1870, but his next-door neighbour, John Medcalf, remained there until after 1876. The two new houses had a series of owners.

(iv) Northenden Road from the 'Legh Arms' to the boundary

Existing properties
Matilda White, a widow born in Cheshire in *1809, was the licensee of the 'Legh Arms' from 1861 to 1867. After a short gap, George Geisser ran it for four years. Born in France in *1845, he had come to England and married a girl

131

from Manchester. In 1875 he moved away and the 'Legh Arms' was sold to a new owner, James Taylor.

Michael Potter stayed at 'Roundland House' until 1867, when he and his family moved out. There were a number of tenants over the following ten years. Thomas Marsland remained at Victoria Farm. This was now a market garden and the house was named 'Victoria Cottage'. 'Yew Tree Cottage' had a change of ownership in 1873 when William Hickman moved to Hereford Street. The new owner and resident was Joseph Leech.

From 1865 Edward Massey ran the 'Nag's Head', at the corner of Wythenshawe Road. He was born in Baguley in *1835. Across the road Sarah Gratrix still dispensed beer and ale at premises which later became the 'Lindow Tavern' until she died in 1877. Most of the land of the Gratrix farm down Sandbach Road had been sold in 1860; the few acres remaining were run by William Gratrix until 1869; there were several tenants in the following years. William was born in Broughton (Lancashire) in *1800. Robert Marsland left 'Beech House' in 1868, and went to live in 'Hiltly', a new house on Walton Road. He was followed at 'Beech House' by William Golding, a corn agent born in Wisbech in *1840. Roylance's Farm continued to be run by John Heywood until his death in 1869. It then devolved to his son, who was also called John (*1840-1906). He was born in Ashton-on-Mersey.

New properties

The cottage next to 'Roundland House' was converted to a terrace of five houses in 1862. They still carry the plaque bearing their name - 'Roundland Terrace'. In the following year Peter Potts, the baker, moved from 'Wallbank Terrace' to a house at the top of Gratrix Lane (it has not been possible to ascertain the exact location). In 1870 William Brickell built a row of ten cottages at right-angles to the main road just east of Gratrix Lane. These were named 'St. Ann's Street'; one of the inhabitants was William Yarwood the blacksmith. Essex Road was laid out between 'Beech House' and 'Boundary House' in the following year. The first nine houses were named 'Edwin Terrace' after the owner of the houses - Edwin Heaps, who lived in the former Leeds house in School Road. Next to them another terrace was completed in the following year. This was named 'Ada Terrace' after Edwin Heaps' daughter. Unusually, 'Edwin Terrace' was numbered 1 to 17 and 'Ada Terrace' 2 to 18, although all the houses were on the same side of the road. Eventually, in the 1950's, Essex Road was extended to Brooklands Road, joining the short road named 'Norris Road'. In 1873 the Primitive Methodist Chapel on Northenden Road was re-built. The minister, the Rev. James Garner, now lived in a new terrace of three houses ('Woodrose Cottages'), which had been built next to the chapel.

(v) South of Northenden Road

The farms lying to the south of Northenden Road were sufficiently far from the centre of Sale for the new housing to have little impact. Shawcross's Farm was managed by John Smith until 1868. The tenancy changed in that year and the new tenant was Ezra Timperley, who was born in Urmston in *1835. He had one man and two boys to help him run the farm. The two parts of Woodiwiss's Farm were still managed by John Hampson and another person. From 1863 this other person was William Walkden. Holly Hey was rented by John E. Wright from 1870. He was born in Cheadle in *1820 and died in 1890.

William Bardsley rented Renshaw's Farm until his death in 1876.

APPENDIX I
Farms in Sale

Details are given here of most of the farms in Sale. The only farms omitted are a few which disappeared early in the nineteenth century. In the case of the larger farms, more information is given with a complete list of tenant farmers between 1806 and 1876. Biographical details of many of the tenant farmers are given in the main body of the book.

Astle's Farm was situated to the east of Rutland Lane. In 1806 it belonged to John Astle (or 'Astley') and covered 31 acres. The main fields were in two parts, with another farm (owned by Lord Stamford) in between. From 1820 the four fields to the east were managed by the tenant of Lord Stamford's farm. The tenant farmer of the western part from 1820 to 1843 was Thomas Chadwick. When John Astle's daughter Mary died in 1850(?), the farmhouse and the fields round it were bought by Edmund Howarth and became a market garden. The farmhouse was now 'The Oaks'. It was bought by James Worthington in 1864 and became part of the Old Hall estate. The eastern part (23 acres) was still being listed separately as 'Late Astle's' in 1876.

Atkinson's Farm was situated on Cross Street. It belonged to Joseph Atkinson of 'Ashfield'. The old farmhouse is now known as 'Eyebrow Cottage' and the fields (24 acres) lay on both sides of School Road. By 1844 the area had increased to 36 acres, but as more and more houses were built after the opening of the railway, the area of the farm diminished, until in 1876 it covered only 5 acres.

Tenant farmers:
Thomas Haslam	1806-12
Elizabeth Haslam	1813-20
Thomas Richardson	1821-65
(W. Joynson)	1866-70
Thomas Lee	1871-after 1876

Robert Barlow's Farm covered 8½ acres near the junction of Northenden Road and Old Hall Road. The farmhouse was situated behind the present shops between Wilkinson Street and Old Hall Road. From 1831 to 1848 the farm was run by John Kelsall. In 1876 the 5½ acres were rented by James Williamson.

Samuel Barlow's Farm was also near the junction of Northenden Road and Marsland Road. The farmhouse was situated behind the present-day shops at the end of Conway Road, and the three fields (6 acres) extended to the south. From 1848 to 1871 the farm was run first by John Kelsall and then by his son,

Jonathan. From 1871 the 5 acres were rented by William Baldwin.

Baxter's Farms. The Baxter family owned two farms in Sale. See 'Moor Nook Farm' and 'Priory Farm'.

Beech Farm ('Woodiwiss's Farm') belonged to Charles White in 1806. Covering 66½ acres, it lay on the southern edge of Sale, and was bordered by Baguley Brook. The farm buildings were reached by going down Baguley Lane and were situated on the east side of the modern Croft Road, between the modern Kershaw Avenue and Kenyon Avenue. In 1809 the farm was sold. The main part went to the Rev. Harrop, but 20 acres were sold to Henry Baxter who owned Priory Farm. Eighteen years later the Rev. Harrop's part (45 acres) was sold again, this time to Francis Woodiwiss, who also bought the Rev. Harrop's portion of Lime Tree Farm at the same time. Beech Farm thus became one of the largest farms in Sale at 100 acres. The two parts were managed by two separate tenant farmers. In 1876 the total area of the farm was 73 acres.

Tenant farmers:
John Chadwick	1806-10
John Garner	1811-22
John Hampson & Edward Gresty	1823- c. 1851
John Hampson & James Credland	1856-61
John Hampson & William Walkden	1863-after 1876

Broad Lane Farm (44 acres) belonged to G.J. Legh. In 1847 the farm lands were sold, mostly to Samuel Brooks, who added them to Temple Farm. John Whitehead moved to Manor Farm (he had been running both farms for four years). The farmhouse on Broad Road (probably rebuilt) became a residence ('Yew Tree Cottage') which survives today.

Tenant farmers:
John Whitehead (senior)	1806-1838
John Whitehead (junior)	1838-47

Brogden's Farm see 'Higson's Farm'

Brooklands Farm (also known as 'Marsland's Farm' and later as 'Hillkirk's Farm') was owned by Lawrence Wright. In 1806 the Marslands had been tenant farmers for over thirty years. The farm lay to the south of Marsland Road, and was one of the largest farms in Sale at 135 acres. The Wright family sold the farm to Samuel Brooks around 1854 and it still covered 140 acres in 1876. The farm buildings were situated on the curve of the modern Framingham Road, between Acrefield and Kirklands. They survived until around 1960.

Tenant farmers:
Edward Marsland	c.1775-1818
Robert Marsland	1818-1857
Robert Cookson	1858-1865
George Fletcher	1866
Roger Hillkirk	1867-80

Chadwick's Farm see 'Beech Farm'

Chapel Lane Farm covered 10 acres, and was owned by G.J. Legh. It was sold to Samuel Brooks in 1847. The farmhouse stood where the Excelsior Club now stands.

In 1844 the area of the farm was 21 acres, but housing development in the 1860's and 1870's reduced the area until in 1876 the farm covered only 3½ acres.

Three of the long-staying tenants were:
Thomas Edwards	1813-1831
Abraham Hewitt	c.1833-47
John Marsland	1848-77

Clark's Hey was a small farm between Broad Road and the canal. It was owned by the Heward family, who also owned Manor Farm on Cross Street. In 1876 the area of the farm was 8½ acres, nearly exactly the same as it had been seventy years previously. The farm buildings were reached by a private lane opposite the end of Irlam Road.

Two of the longer-staying tenant farmers were:
John Sutherland	1827-44
William Smith	1844-75

Dane Road Farm was owned by G.J.Legh in 1806, and covered 30 acres. In 1847 it was sold to Samuel Brooks, who appears to have incorporated it into Temple Farm. The old farmhouse then housed farm labourers. It survives today, although it has recently been much altered.

Tenant farmers:
George Woodall	1806-12
John Singleton	1813-19
Peter Singleton	1820-22
John Singleton	1823-47

Fairy Lane Farm see 'Oak Farm'

George Gratrix's Farm was originally owned by Lord Stamford. In 1828 he sold it to George Gratrix, and the farm was then known as 'Gratrix's Farm' in spite of the fact that there was another 'Gratrix' farm (owned by Peter Gratrix) only 600 yards to the south. The farm lay between Astle's Farm and Sale New Hall, and the farmhouse was reached by means of a short lane running off Fairy Lane. The nine fields covered 24 acres. The farm was sold in 1876 to R.L. Reade. The farmhouse later became 'Shevington House'.

Tenant farmers:
Ralph Barlow jun.	1806-20
James Brown	1822-39
Joseph Morgan	1840-68
James Morgan	1868-after 1876

Peter Gratrix's Farm The Gratrix family lands lay to the east of Sandbach Road. In 1806 the farm covered 32 acres, a figure which still applied fifty years later. In 1860 however most of the land was sold to John Kelsall of Holly Hey, and only 6 acres remained.

Tenant farmers:
Edward Gratrix	c.1775-
Peter Gratrix sen.	1836-39
Peter Gratrix jun.	1839-41
John Gratrix	1841-58
John Mee	1859-61
William Gratrix	1862-69
Richard Brooks	1870-72
Thomas Morris	1873-after 1876

Higson's Farms There were two Higson farms at Moor Nook. One (11 acres) was rented by John Higson junior. After his death in 1806, it was managed by successive members of the Higson family until James Higson took over in 1827. He continued to run the farm even after it had been sold to John Brogden in 1847. John Brogden's widow sold it to Joseph Clarke (of Lime Grove) in 1873. In 1876 the area was 19½ acres.

Tenant farmers:
John Higson junior	1806
Sarah Higson	1806-1825
James Higson	1827-53?
Charles Garner	1853?-68
John Gough	1868-after 1876

The other farm (28 acres) was on a long-term lease from Lord Stamford to John Higson senior in 1806. In 1844 it still covered 21 acres.

Tenant farmers:
John Higson senior	1806-1814

George Brown   1821-25
Peter Brown   1826-40
James Higson   1840-53?

Hillkirk's Farm see 'Brooklands Farm'

Holly Hey was a triangular 5-acre field right on the township boundary at the end of the track which later became Sandbach Road. Originally it was part of the Sale Old Hall estate, but was purchased by James Woodall, junior, around 1835, and a house erected on the plot. In 1860 he retired and his successor was John Kelsall, who bought most of the neighbouring Gratrix Farm.

Lime Tree Farm ('Shawcross's Farm') in 1806 was the second largest farm in Sale (119 acres). It belonged jointly to George J. Legh and William Egerton. The farm buildings were situated in the bend of Baguley Lane (now the playing field of Lime Tree Primary School). The farm was sold to Matthew Shawcross in 1807. Two years later he sold almost two thirds of it, retaining only 42 acres. 51 acres on the west side of Baguley Lane were bought by the Rev. Robert Harrop, 20½ acres between the Priory and the River Mersey were bought by George Ashton and 5½ acres by John Whitehead. In 1827 the executors of the Rev. Harrop sold his portion to Francis Woodiwiss and the Ashton portion was sold to John White. In 1844 Shawcross's Farm covered 46 acres, a figure which still applied in 1876.

Tenant farmers:
Jonathan Renshaw   1806-13
Peter Gratrix   1814-25
William Dewsbury   1826-50
John Smith   1850-68
Ezra Timperley   1869-after 1876

Lyth's Farm see 'Oak Farm'

Manor Farm belonged to the Heyward family. The farm buildings were on Cross Street, just north of Dane Road. In 1806 the farm consisted of 29 acres. In 1863 the area of the farm was 33½ acres, but the building of houses in the late 1860's and early 1870's reduced this to 9 acres in 1876. From 1866 it appears to have been run by Thomas Lee together with Atkinson's Farm.

Tenant farmers:
Peter Heward (owner)   1806-17
Thomas Heward   1818-42
Joseph Heward   1843
John Whitehead   1843-66
(John Worthington and later Isaiah Litherland lived at the farmhouse after

1866, but they were not farmers)

Marsland's Farm (Brooklands) see 'Brooklands Farm'

Marsland's Farm (Rutland Lane) belonged to James Marsland. In 1806 the farm covered 39 acres, mostly on the east side of Rutland Lane, extending from Wythenshawe Road to the River Mersey. In 1844 his son John still owned 36 acres, but by 1851 this had been reduced to 16½ acres. The area round Rutland Lane had been sold first to Edmund Howarth as 'Sale Lodge Farm', then in 1864 to James Worthington as 'Sale Old Hall Farm'. James Marsland was still running the farm (40 acres) for James Worthington in 1876.

Moor Cottage Farm covered 5 acres at the junction of Marsland Road and Derbyshire Road. In 1844 it belonged to Joseph Moore and was rented by James Bardsley, who also rented what remained of Pinfold Farm. Later it was known as 'Moorside Gardens' and was rented for thirty years by the Alcock family. In 1888 it was purchased by Thomas Walkden, whose descendants bequeathed it to Sale Council in 1970 as 'Walkden Gardens'.

Moor Nook Farm in 1806 was owned by George Ashton, and covered 20 acres. In 1826 it devolved to the Baxter family. By 1844 its area had increased to 44½ acres, mainly by the purchase of John Garner's six fields (21 acres) on the north-east side of Derbyshire Road South. Moor Nook farmhouse was situated on the south-west side of Derbyshire Lane South opposite the present petrol station. In 1876 the farm's area was 44½ acres.

Tenant famers:
John Davenport	c.1775-1819
Samuel Davenport	1820-23
George Brown	1823-41
William Brown	1842-71
James Simpson	1871-after 1876

New Farm belonged to the Taylors of Riddings Hall, Timperley. In 1806 it covered 69 acres. There were no farm buildings until later, possibly when Richard Howarth took over the tenancy in 1823. The buildings lay on Washway Road, immediately south of 'Woodheys'. Over the years some of the land was sold off for housing, but in 1876 the farm still covered 49 acres.

Tenant farmers:
James Goodier	1806-22
Richard Howarth	1823-42
Martha Howarth	1842-44
John Carter	1845-51
George Whitelegg	1856-7

Thomas Whitelegg　　　　　　　　1858-64
James Blain　　　　　　　　　　　1865-after 1876

New Hall Farm ('Sale New Hall') covered 77 acres in 1806, and belonged to the White family of Sale Priory. The Hall, which dates from the 1650's, was situated on New Hall Lane, and most of the fields lay between it and the township boundary. The purchase of neighbouring land enlarged the area to 124½ acres in 1844, and in 1876 it was still 119 acres.

Tenant farmers:
William Cookson (sen.)	1806-21
William Cookson (jun.)	1821-25
Samuel Faulkner	1826
Martha Faulkner	1827-30
(Exors. of Martha Faulkner	1831-42)
Thomas Barlow	1843-52
Thomas Pearson	1856-58
Charles Leigh	1859-60
Thomas Leigh	1861-67
John Wood	1868-after 1876

Oak Farm ('Lyth's Farm') lay right on the eastern boundary of Sale township at the end of Fairy Lane. In 1806 it covered 18½ acres, and at that time there were no farm buildings. Presumably it was then part of a Northenden farm. Originally belonging to John Schofield, in 1841 it was sold to Samuel Lyth, and from then on was often referred to as 'Lyth's Farm'. It still covered 18 acres in 1876. The farm buildings were situated right at the end of Fairy Lane.

Tenant farmers:
John Scho(le)field (owner)	1806-1830
John Strettell	1831-41
James Smith	1842-50
Thomas Smith	1851-after 1876

Pearson's Farm covered 15 acres on the west side of Priory Road. The farm buildings stood nearly opposite the road to the modern Abbot's Court. The area was increased to 28½. acres by the purchase of land from Lady Thorold and Charles White, and in 1876 the farm still covered 21½ acres.

Tenant farmers:
James Hulme	1806
John Hulme	1807-8
Joseph Roberts	1809-14
James Goodier	1815-17
James Gratrix	1818-27

William Nelson	1828-30
John Hancock	1831-47
Samuel Hancock	1847-54
John Ridyard	1854-63
Charles Morgan	1864-after 1876

Pinfold Farm covered 25 acres on the north side of Dane Road. In 1806 it was rented from Lord Stamford by Ashton Kelsall. It was bought by Ashton's son, James, in 1828. After James's death in 1838, his widow Sarah sold most of the land to Samuel Brooks and Thomas Barlow. In 1844 the latter's 12 acres were farmed by James Bardsley, who also rented Moor Cottage Farm.

Priory Farm belonged to the Baxter family. It covered 41 acres in 1806, and was farmed by James Hulme. In 1810 the farm area was increased to 67 acres by the purchase of four fields of Beech Farm near the southern boundary of Sale. The area of the farm was still 67 acres in 1876.

Tenant farmers:
James Hulme	c.1775-1806
John Hulme	1807-25
Thomas Bancroft	1825-40
Peter Brown	1840-74
Alice Brown	1874-after 1876

Renshaw's Farm covered 10 acres on the south side of Northenden Road, between Baguley Lane and Gratrix Lane. It was formed from fields purchased from the Sale Old Hall Estate in 1824 by James Renshaw. The tenant farmer from 1849-73 was William Bardsley, who also managed 33 acres of Beech Farm.

Roylance's Farm covered 15 acres at the top of Baguley Lane. It belonged to the Leghs, who sold it to Samuel Brooks in 1847. The area was 12½ acres in 1876.

Tenant farmers:
William Roylance	c.1775-1819
Thomas Renshaw	1820-28
John Cordingley	1829-45
John Heywood sen.	1845-69
John Heywood jun.	1869-after 1876

Sale Lodge Farm see 'Marsland's Farm' (Rutland Lane)

Sale New Hall Farm see 'New Hall Farm'

Sale Old Hall Farm see 'Marsland's Farm (Rutland Lane)'

Shawcross's Farm see 'Lime Tree Farm'

Temple Farm belonged to Lord Stamford. In 1806 it covered 22½ acres. The farm buildings still survive near the junction of Temple Road and Dane Road. In 1830 Lord Stamford sold it to Samuel Brooks. By 1863 the area had increased to 154 acres by the purchase of lands formerly belonging to other farms in the vicinity (e.g. Broad Road Farm, Dane Road Farm and Pinfold Farm). In 1876 the farm's area was still 153 acres.

Tenant farmers:
Richard Knight	1806-7
Ralph Dean	1808-9
Mary Dean	1810-12
James Cheshire	1812-20
Samuel Barlow	1821-3
Alice Barlow	1824-30
Thomas Barlow	1831-43
Joseph Cordingley	1843-after 1876

Victoria Farm was a smallholding of 5 acres on the north side of Northenden Road, near the junction with Baguley Road. The tenant farmer for 26 years from 1844 was Thomas Marsland.

Wallbank Farm belonged to the White family of Sale Priory. It covered 51½ acres in 1806. The farm buildings were situated on the west side of Old Hall Road, opposite Sale Old Hall. By 1844 the farm's area had doubled to 108 acres and in 1876 the area was 83 acres.

Tenant farmers:
William Alderley	1806-12
Samuel Alderley	1812-c.1853
Jabez Alderley	c.1853-67
John Wood	1868-after 1876

Wardle's Farm was formed in the 1830's from the enclosure of Sale Moor. It covered 10 acres, which gradually decreased as houses were built on Wardle Road. Upon the death of the last tenant farmer (Thomas Renshaw) in 1866, the farm lands were sold and the farmhouse rebuilt as 'Wardle House'.

Washway Farm lay at the southern edge of Sale, just north of Siddall's Bridge. With an area of 64 acres, it belonged to Lord Stamford until he sold it to Joseph Clarke in 1813. In 1876 it covered 40 acres.

Tenant farmers:
Edward Pearson	1806
Philip Derbyshire	1807-21
Joseph Hampson	1822-51
Samuel Hancock	1856-62
Joseph Davies	1863-68
William Owen	1870-after 1876

Waterside Farm belonged to William Whitelegg of Northenden. It covered 24 acres in the north-east corner of Sale. Its area was still 27½ acres in 1876.

Tenant farmers:
John Alderley	1806-27
John Gresty	1831
Peter Gratrix jr.	1836-42
James Carter	1843-49
Samuel Woodall	1850-69
Thomas Smith	1870-after 1876

Whitehall Farm was owned by Lord Stamford. It was leased by William Williamson of Ashton New Hall, who also owned a number of fields in the vicinity. When the farm was sold to Samuel Brooks in 1847 the dual nature of the farm continued. The total area in 1806 was 31½ acres. By 1876 this had been reduced to 13½ acres.

Tenant farmers:
John Moss	1806-14
James Higson	1815-18
James Royle	1819
Thomas Royle	1825-6
Thomas Renshaw	1827-54
William Bridge jr.	1856-8
Richard Hayman	1859-63
John Williamson	1864-5
Thomas Greenall	1866
Edward Whitteron	1867
John Little	1868-after 1876

Whitehead's Farm was a small farm on the south side of Northenden Road. The farmhouse stood nearly opposite Yew Tree Cottage. John Whitehead (of Broad Road Farm) owned a 4-acre field here in 1806, and his holding was increased to 14 acres by the purchase of land from Lime Tree Farm. In 1876 the farm was run by William Whitehead.

Williamson's Farm see 'Whitehall Farm'

Woodiwiss's Farm see 'Beech Farm'

Wright's Farm see 'Brooklands Farm'

APPENDIX II
Large Houses

This is a list of the older large houses in Sale. Biographical details of many of the occupants will be found in the main body of the book.

Readers may notice that the information given below differs from that quoted in the book *Cedric II*. The reason is that we now have access to a large number of documents which were not available to Henry Hulme ('Cedric') when he wrote his book.

Ashfield, originally the home of the Irlam family, stood near the junction of Chapel Road and Cross Street. It was bought by Joseph Atkinson in 1793 and his grandson sold it to William Joynson in 1875. It was demolished in 1908.

Occupants:
Joseph Atkinson	1793-1818
David Scott	1820-31
empty?	1836-42
William Joynson	1843-after 1876

Beechfield, on Washway Road, was built for Richard Lane in 1843. It was demolished around 1960.

Occupants:
Richard Lane	1843-58
John Bellhouse	1859-63
Isabella Bellhouse	1863-69
Walter Bellhouse	1869-after 1876

Broadoaks was built by Samuel Roebuck in 1851. It was a very large semi-detached house. It was demolished in 1920.

Occupants:
Richard Zahn	1851-75
Mrs. Zahn	1875-after 1876
John Pilling	1851?-1860
Alfred Midwood	1861-71
Richard Hardwick	1871-after 1876

Miry Gate House see Priory Gate House

The Old Manor House was situated next to 'Eyebrow Cottage' on Cross Street. It was demolished in the 1970's.

Occupants:
John Moore	1806-28
empty	1829
Jane Bellott	1830-49
empty	1850
Oswald Grundy	1851-56
Mary Denman	1857-8
Rev. Alfred Ellis	1859-64
Ellen Ogden	1865-after 1876

Priory Gate House on Dane Road existed in the eighteenth-century. Originally named 'Miry Gate House', in 1806 it belonged to Lord Stamford. He sold it in 1828 to Samuel Brooks who probably then rebuilt it. It was demolished in 1936-7.

Occupants:
John Leebridge	1806
William Leebridge	1807-13
Samuel Smith	1814-18
John Siddall	1821
William Siddall	1826-31
Sarah Siddall	1836
John Brogden	1837*-59
John Herriott	1859-61
William Shore	1862-64
John Woodhead	1865-66
Isaac Hoyle	1867-71
John Coulson	1872-73
Alice Kay	1873-after 1876
	* see p.78

Sale Bank was built for Samuel Roebuck on Washway Road in 1837. It was demolished in 1913-4.

Occupants:
Samuel Roebuck	1837-65
Hannah Roebuck	1865-74
William Brakespear	1874-after 1876

Sale Cottage was situated on Old Hall Road. It dated from the eighteenth century. It was privately owned by most of its occupants. When John Duncan left in 1878 it was rebuilt into three terraced houses.

Occupants:
John Cookson	1806-17

Jonathan Hatfield	1818-23
Charles Wood	1824-31
R. Leigh Trafford	1836-46
William Tebbutt	1847-55
James Kennedy	1856-61
William Tebbutt	1861-62
John Duncan	1865-after 1876

Sale Heys Cottage also dated from the eighteenth century. Situated behind the Big Pit on Washway Road, it belonged to the Taylors of Riddings Hall. It was demolished in 1928-9.

Occupants:
John Whitehead	1806-28
Charles Rampling	1829-30
James Hammond	1831
Joseph Russell	1838
George Crossley	1840
empty	1841
Martin Just	1843-44
David Bellhouse	1845-66
Edward T. Bellhouse	1866-after 1876

Sale Lodge was built for Edmund Howarth in 1836. It was situated to the south-east of the Old Hall. It is now the club-house of Sale Golf Club.

Occupants:
Edmund Howarth sen.	1836-55
Edmund Howarth jun.	1855-59
William H. Bradley	1859-65
John Stott Milne	1866-after 1876

Sale New Hall see 'Farms'

Sale Old Hall dated from around 1600, although this building probably replaced an earlier one. It was situated near the junction of Rifle Road and Old Hall Road. It was sold by J.G. Legh to John Moore in 1807; he in turn sold it Mary Worthington in 1840. It was demolished in 1920-1.

Occupants:
Samuel Norris	1780-91
Alice Norris	1791-1803
Thomas Mort	1803-12
empty	1813
Edward Hanson	1814-17

J.A. Bury	1818-21
John Moore	1822-39
Mary Worthington	1840-46
Edward Lyon	1847-51
John Peel	1855-59
Matthew Curtis	1859-62
James Worthington	1863-after 1876

Sale Priory on Dane Road was built by Dr.Thomas White in 1711. It was demolished in 1932.

Occupants:

Dr. Charles White	1776-1813
Capt. John White	1813-1828
William Newton	1829
W. Newton's widow	1830
Charles Roylance	1831-39
John F. Foster	1840-c.53
empty	1856
Gustav Schutz	1857-61
John M. Dunlop	1862-66
William R. Jolly	1867-after 1876

Woodheys was built on Washway Road by Samuel Brooks in 1857. It is now a private sports club.

Occupants:

John A. Critchley	1857-66
Harold Lees	1867-69
Alexander W. Smith	1870-after 1876

APPENDIX III
Origins of street names

Beaufort Road, 104
Broad Road, 75
Chapel Road, 32
Clarendon Crescent, 75
Cross Street, 14, 31
Dane Road, 73
Dean Lane, 73
Derbyshire Road, 34, 37
Dudley Road, 83
Friars Road, 58
George's Road, 104
Hart Lane, 118
Hereford Street, 58
Hope Road, 34
Irlam Road, 90
Jackson Street, 91
Marsland Road, 95
Moor Lane, 118
Morley's Lane, 53
Moss's Lane, 34, 95
New Lane, 96

Norris Road, 111
Orchard Place, 57
Poplar Grove, 49
Priory Road, 74
Raglan Road, 102, 108
Roebuck Lane, 39
School Road, 32
Sibson Road, 58
Skaife Road, 85
South Grove, 49
Springfield Road, 42
Tebbutt's Lane, 126
Temple Road, 34, 75
Wardle Road, 37
Warrener Street, 44
Washway Road, 14
West Grove, 49
Whitehall Road, 95
Wilson Street, 55
Woodlands Road, 91
Wythenshawe Road, 17

BIBLIOGRAPHY

Primary Sources
Cheshire Land Tax returns, 1780-1831
Sale Poor Rate books, 1836-1888
Census returns 1841, 1851, 1861, 1871, 1881
Census summaries 1801, 1811, 1821, 1831, 1841, 1851, 1861, 1871, 1881
Tithe map and apportionment for Sale (1844)
Parish registers for St. Martin's, Ashton-on-Mersey
Brooklands Cemetery monumental inscriptions
Sale Township Vestry minutes 1805-1876
Sale Urban District Council minutes 1867-76
G. Legh Estate map (1801), Trafford Local Studies Centre
W. Wilson map of Sale (1860), Trafford Local Studies Centre
E. Mason Pre-Enclosure map of Sale (1806), Trafford Local Studies Centre
Post-Enclosure map of Sale (1807)
Ordnance Survey maps, 1848, 1876, 1899, 1911, 1934, 1973

Directories
Pigott, *Manchester, Salford & vicinities*, 1836,1838, 1840
Pigott and Slater, *Manchester, Salford & vicinities*, 1841, 1843
Slater, *Manchester, Salford & vicinities*, 1845, 1848, 1851, 1852
Slater, *Directory of Cheshire*, 1844, 1850-1
Bagshaw, *Commercial Directory of Cheshire*, 1850, 1857
Slater, *Commercial Directory of Northern England*, 1848
Whelan & Co, *A New Alphabetical & Classified Directory of Manchester & Salford*, 1853
Slater, *Directory of the Northern Counties*, 1855
White, *History & Gazeteer of Cheshire*, 1860
Morris, *Commercial Directory of Cheshire*, 1864, 1874
Kelly, *Post Office Directory of Chehsire*, 1857, 1864, 1878
Slater/Kelly, *Manchester & suburbs*, 1888-1942

Secondary Sources
Printed
H.W. Atkinson, *The Families of Atkinson of Roxby (Lincs.) & Thorne and Dearman of Braithwaite*, self-pub. 1933 (copy in Manchester Central Library)
D.R. Bellhouse, *David Bellhouse & Sons, Manchester*, self-pub, 1992 (copy in Manchester Central Library)
A. Brook & B. Haworth, *Boomtown Manchester*, The Portico Library, 1993
H.M. Colvin, *A Biographical Dictionary of English Architects, 1660-1840*, Yale University Press, 1978
T.A.Coward, *Cheshire Traditions & History*, Methuen & Co., 1932

F. Dixon, *The Manchester, South Junction & Altrincham Railway*, Oakwood Press, 2nd. edition, 1994
C. Hadfield & G. Biddle, *The Canals of North West England*, David & Charles, 1970
V. Hainsworth, *Looking Back at Sale*, Willow Publishing, 1983
F.C. Mather, *After the Canal Duke*, Oxford University Press, 1970
G. Ormerod, *History of the County Palatine and City of Chester*, G. Routledge & Sons, 1882
J. Pipkin, *Cross Street Chapel, Cheshire*, H. Rawson & Co., Manchester, 1925
M.D. Whitehorn, *The Story of Sale United Reformed Church 1805-1985*, Sale United Reformed Church, 1985
The Chadderton Mummy, or the Ghost of Birchen Bower, Chadderton History Society, 1993
Sale Wesleyan Methodist Church 1853-1953, centenary booklet, 1953
Transactions of the Lancashire & Cheshire Antiquarian Society, 1891
Sale Illustrated, Spring 1953
Sale Pioneer, March 1948
The Sphinx, 22 August, 1868

General Index

(See separate indices for surnames and house names)

Albert Road, 70
Alice Street, 62
Arnesby Avenue, 74
Ashton & Sale Volunteer Force, 9, 26
Ashton New Hall, 95, 143
Assembly Rooms, 84
Astle's Farm, 117, 122, 126, 131, 134
Atkinson's Farm, 72, 78, 82, 87, 134

Back Lane, 75
Baguley, 104, 109, 111
Baguley Brook, 9, 11, 93, 111, 120
Baguley Lane, 96, 118, 120, 138, 141
Baguley Road, 11, 20, 117, 123,
Bank Street, 89
Banks, 57
Barlow Farms, 34, 37, 59, 96, 99, 105, 114, 134
Barrow Brook, 9, 11
Baxter's Farm, 74, 80, 84, 105, 135
Beaufort Avenue, 113
Beaufort Road, 103, 104
Beech Farm, 120, 124, 128, 133, 135
Belfort Hotel, 90
Big Pit, 93, 147
Boats, 12, 14
Boggart Lane, 104
Bowdon, 14
'Bridge Inn', 83, 87
Bridgewater Canal, 12, 21, 83, 93
Bridgewater Street, 55
Britannia Grove, 43, 61
Broad Lane Chapel, 16, 41, 63, 81
Broad Lane Farm, 20, 75, 82, 84, 135
Broad Road, 75, 81, 84, 89
Broadoaks Road, 54
Brogden's Farm, 52, 105, 114, 135
Brook Street, 89
Brooklands, 47
Brooklands Bridge, 95, 97
Brooklands Cemetery, 17, 26, 27, 109
Brooklands Crescent, 111, 113

Brooklands Cricket Club, 95
Brooklands Farm, 37, 95, 102, 104, 108, 135
Brooklands Grove, 113
Brooklands Hotel, 66, 104, 108, 109
Brooklands Road, 90, 104, 109, 132
Brooklands School, 68
Brooklands Station, 111
Brooks's Drive, 104
'Bull's Head', 31, 32, 36, 40, 55, 57
Button Brook, 11
Bythell's Bridge, 11, 107
Bythell's Lane, 32

Canal Street, 55
Carrington Moss, 11
'Carter's Arms', 128
Chadwick's Farm, 21, 74, 96, 120, 124, 136
Chapel Lane Farm, 20, 40, 122, 136
Chapel Road, 32, 36, 40, 55
Chemical works, 88
Cheltenham Drive, 61
Churches, 14
Clarendon Crescent, 75, 80, 84, 89
Clarendon Road, 43, 46, 63
Clark's Hey, 73, 75, 77, 81, 84, 89, 136
Co-operative Store, 57
Congregational Chapel - see Independent Chapel
Conway Road, 96, 114
Cow Lane, 74
Craven Terrace, 45, 62
Cross Street, 14, 31, 40, 52, 55, 72, 78, 82, 87, 145
Cross Street Chapel, 16, 32, 121
Crossford Bridge, 11, 14
Council offices, 56

Dane Lodge Hotel, 62
Dane Road, 11, 34, 72, 78, 80, 82, 146, 148

152

Dane Road Farm, 20, 74, 82, 87-88, 136
Davenport Lane, 117
Dean Lane, 72
Derbyshire Road, 11, 34, 37, 52, 56, 69, 105
Drill Hall, 55, 56
Dunham Massey Hall, 20

Eden Place, 55
Egerton Street, 55
Eliza Street, 55
Elizabeth Street, 59
Enclosures, 11, 36, 75, 97, 122
Era Street, 44, 65
Essex Road, 132
Events, 26
Evesham Grove, 75

Fairy Lane, 117, 122, 126, 131
Finch Lane, 34, 75
Fleam, The, 11, 95, 107
Four Lane Ends, 75, 117, 125
Freetown, 47
Friars Road, 58

Gas Co., Stretford, 26
George's Road, 95, 104
Glebelands Road, 11, 34
Gratrix Lane, 84, 118, 120, 123, 132
Gratrix's Farm, 88, 117, 122, 128, 131-32, 136
Grove, The, 113
Guidepost, 82, 118, 123, 127

Hale Barns, 104, 121
Hart Lane, 118, 123
Hayfield Street, 43
Hereford Street, 58
Hesketh Road, 87
Highfield, 66-67
High Legh, 20
Higson's Corner, 34, 95
Higson's Farm, 95, 99, 105, 137
Hillkirk's Farm - see Brooklands Farm
Holford Street, 14
Holly Hey, 123, 128, 133, 138

Holmefield, 65
Hope Road, 11, 44, 58, 64
House Names, 17
Howarth's Lane, 126
Hunting establishment, 88

Independent Chapel, 16, 32, 41, 44, 52, 55
Irlam Road, 11, 90-91

Jackson Street, 90
Jackson's Ferry, 115
Jackson's Ford, 115
John Street, 59
'Jolly Carter', 86, 127
Joynson Street, 56

King Street, 87

Land Ownership, 19
'Legh Arms', 34, 37, 47, 80, 117, 118, 123, 125, 127, 130-32
Lime Tree Farm, 20, 96, 120, 124, 128, 132, 138
'Lindow Tavern', 118, 120, 124, 128, 132
'Little Brooklands Hotel', 104, 108, 113
Local Government, 16, 26
Lords of the Manor, 16, 78, 121
Lyth's Farm - see Oak Farm

Manor Farm, 73, 81-82, 84, 87, 138
Market Place, 55
Marsland Grove, 113
Marsland Road, 11, 34, 47, 93, 95, 97, 102, 108
Marsland's Bridge, 34, 47, 95, 109
Marsland's Farm, 117, 122, 126, 139
Mason Street, 55
Mersey, River, 9, 32, 72-74, 87, 115, 121, 125, 130, 139
Methodists - see Primitive & Wesleyan
Miry Gate Farm, 84
Miry Lane, 74
Montague Road, 51, 52, 68
Moor Cottage Farm, 97, 139

153

Moor Lane, 34, 118
Moor Nook, 20, 95, 99, 105, 114
Moor Nook Farm, 80, 95, 99, 105, 114, 139
Moorfield Gardens, 68, 108, 139
Moorside Nurseries, 97
Morley's Lane, 53
Moss's Lane, 34, 95
MSJ&AR - see Railway

'Nag's Head', 127, 132
New Farm, 93, 97, 101, 107, 139
New Lane, 96
Norris Road, 132
North Street, 49
Northenden Road, 11, 34, 37, 43, 59, 86, 118, 120, 123, 127-28, 130-32, 142

Oak Farm, 118, 122, 127, 140
Oak Road, 47, 64, 68, 127
Occupations, 24
Old Hall Road, 74, 115, 117, 121, 125-26, 130, 146, 147
Orchard Place, 57

Parishes, 14, 59
Parr's Bank, 57
Partington Place, 42
Pearson's Farm, 74, 80, 84, 88, 101, 140
Pepper Hill, 74, 80, 82, 83
Perseverance Street, 114
Pinfold, 74
Pinfold Farm, 74, 82, 88, 139, 141
Police Station, 55
Poor, The, 17
Poor House, 95
Poplar Grove, 49, 68
Population, 23
Presbyterian Chapel, 16, 32, 62
Primitive Methodists, 123, 132
Priory Farm, 74, 88, 141
Priory Road, 74, 80, 84, 88
Property Ownership, 19

'Queen's Hotel', 34, 46, 64

Radford Farm, 103, 109
Raglan Road, 11, 93, 97, 102, 108
Railway, 27, 40, 47, 65, 101, 107, 109
Renshaw's Farm, 123, 129, 133, 141
Riddings Hall, 139, 147
Road Names, 17
Roads, 14
Roebuck Lane, 39, 54, 71
Roman Catholic Chapel, 64
Roylance's Farm, 97, 118, 132, 141
Rutland Lane, 117, 122, 126, 131, 139

Sale Botanical Gardens, 108
Sale Bridge, 16, 34
Sale Cricket Club, 75, 91
Sale Golf Club, 121, 147
Sale Grammar School, 109
Sale Green, 115, 121, 125, 127, 130
Sale Hedge, 11
Sale Heys Road, 93, 97
Sale High School, 109
Sale Hotel, 108
Sale Institute, 55
Sale Lodge School, 126, 131
Sale Moor, 11, 26, 35-37, 47, 72, 75, 93, 97
Sandbach Road, 120, 124, 132, 137-38
School - see Township School
School Road, 11, 32, 36, 41, 56
Shawcross's Farm - see Lime Tree Farm
Sibson Road, 42, 57
Siddall's Bridge, 11, 14
Skaife Road, 85
South Grove, 49, 69, 103
South Street, 49
Springfield Road, 42, 56
St. Anne's Church, 16, 26, 45, 59
St. Anne's School, 62
St. Ann's Street, 132
St. John's Church, 109
St. Joseph's, 64
St. Martin's Church, 14, 16, 81-82, 97
St. Paul's Church, 42
Stamford Place, 42, 45-46, 52, 59
Stanley Grove, 42, 56
Stanley Mount, 107

Stanley Terrace, 107
Street lighting, 26
Street numbering, 7, 17
Stromford Brook, 11

Tatton Hall, 20
Tebbutt's Lane, 126
Temple Farm, 75, 80, 88, 96, 142
Temple Road, 34, 39, 46, 63, 75, 80, 82, 84, 89
Thorn Grove, 64
Thorold Grove, 75
Tithes, 16
Topography, 9
Township School, 32, 57
Trinity Chapel, 63
Trinity Road, 70
Turnpike, 14

Union Club, 55
Unitarian Chapel, 16, 32

Vestry, 16, 28
Victoria Farm, 118, 132, 142
'Vine', The, 53, 70

Wallbank Farm, 21, 34, 115, 121, 125, 130-31, 142
Walton Road, 108, 132
Wardle Road, 11, 34, 37, 51, 66, 95, 143
Wardle's Farm, 51, 66, 102, 142

Warrener Street, 44, 62
Washway Farm, 21, 80, 93, 97, 101, 107, 142
Washway Road, 14, 35, 39, 40, 53, 57, 70, 93, 97, 101, 107, 145, 146-47
Water Co., North Cheshire, 26
Waterside, 21, 118, 122
Waterside Farm, 21, 118, 122, 127, 131, 143
Watling Street, 14
Wesleyan Methodists, 16, 41, 43, 52, 57, 81
West Grove, 49. 51, 69
West Street, 49
Wharf Road, 84, 89
Whitehall Farm, 21, 34, 95, 97, 102, 104, 108, 123, 143
Whitehall Road, 95
White's Bridge, 73, 80, 83, 88
White's Monument, 73
Whitehead's Farm, 143
Wickenby Drive, 54
Wilkinson Street, 62
Williamson's Farm - see Whitehall Farm
Wilson Street, 55
Woodiwiss's Farm - see Beech Farm
Woodlands Road, 91
Wright's Farm - see Brooklands Farm
Wythenshawe Road, 17, 117-18, 122, 126, 131

Surname Index

Acton, 63
Aked, 51
Ainsworth, 90
Alcock, 43, 64, 102
Aldcroft, 128
Alderley, 34, 36-37, 41-42, 78, 115, 118, 121-23, 125-27, 130, 142-43
Allen, 51, 68
Alston, 67
Amos, 67
Anderson, 49, 68
Armstrong, 70
Arnold, 83
Ashcroft, 56, 82
Ashford, 71
Ashton, 74, 79, 95, 117, 138-39
Aspinall, 61
Astle, 117
Atkinson, 31-32, 35-37, 42, 58, 72, 102, 134, 145
Auty, 65

Baguley, 64
Baird, 68
Baker, 73
Baldwin, 114, 135
Bancroft, 80, 141
Bardsley, 82, 97, 99, 102, 128, 133, 139, 141
Barker, 68
Barlow, 34, 37, 59, 80, 82, 84, 96, 99, 105, 117, 120, 122, 126, 134, 137, 140-42
Barnes, 88
Barratt, 85
Barrow, 128
Baxendell, 44
Baxter, 70, 103, 135, 139
Bayley, 82
Bellhouse, 12, 22, 101, 107, 111, 145, 147
Bellis, 114
Bellott, 78, 82, 146

Beswick, 73, 85, 89
Binyon, 71
Birchall, 55
Bird, 70
Birkenhead, 53, 70
Blackburn, 51
Blain, 107, 140
Bloor, 21, 44
Boddington, 61
Booth, 20, 69
Bradbury, 44
Bradford, 104, 108
Bradley, 125, 130, 147
Brakespear, 70, 146
Brewer, 52
Brickell, 21, 37, 46, 64, 123, 127-28, 132
Bridge, 51, 66, 102, 143
Briggs, 66
Brindley, 53, 59
Brogden, 22, 41, 78, 83, 105, 107, 111, 113, 137, 146
Brook, 49
Brooke, 109
Brookes, 126
Brooks, 20-21, 40, 45, 52, 55, 78, 80, 82, 88, 97, 101, 104, 107, 109, 111, 127, 130, 135, 136-37, 141-43, 146, 148
Brophy, 56
Brown, 37, 80, 84, 88, 90, 99, 105, 113-14, 137-39, 141
Brownhill, 36-37, 54, 80, 99, 115, 118, 127
Buck, 111
Bundock, 52
Burchardt, 113
Burgess, 39, 89, 113
Bury, 121, 148
Butterfield, 26, 46, 85, 89
Butterworth, 89
Bythell, 37, 39

Campbell, 113
Carter, 78, 83, 101, 127, 139, 143
Cartwright, 49
Chadwick, 120, 122, 126, 135
Chapman, 37, 43
Charnock, 111
Cheetham, 88, 121
Cheshire, 142
Clark, 37, 97
Clarke, 68, 103, 109, 114, 125, 127, 142
Clegg, 42, 65
Clough, 51, 57, 66
Cochrane, 89
Collier, 46, 61
Cookson, 37, 43, 74, 80, 83, 102, 108, 115, 117, 120, 122-24, 127-28, 136, 140, 147
Cordingley, 26, 78, 83-84, 89, 123, 127, 141-42
Corkill, 91
Cort, 45-46, 63
Coulson, 146
Crawley, 64
Credland, 135
Critchley, 68, 101, 107, 148
Crompton, 57, 113
Croom, 56
Cross, 52
Crossley, 147
Crowther, 125
Cuff, 122
Cuffley, 47, 64
Cunningham, 104, 109, 128
Curtis, 125, 148

Dale, 83, 88
Davenport, 95, 99, 117, 126, 131, 139
Davies, 66, 143
Deacon, 61
Dean, 142
De Lannoy, 49
Denman, 82, 103, 146
Denton, 58
Derbyshire, 37, 49, 69, 143
Dewsbury, 118, 124, 128, 138
Dickinson, 36-37, 75

Dowson, 89
Dudley, 83
Duncan, 130, 146-47
Dunlop, 148
Dunn, 61, 69, 71, 84
Dutton, 49, 68

Earl, 43, 84
Edminson, 61, 63
Edwards, 136
Egerton, 20, 115, 120, 124, 138
Ellerback, 111
Ellis, 82, 87, 146
Emmett, 51
Evans, 83, 103
Evison, 42

Farrell, 127
Faulkner, 47, 64, 122, 140
Fereday, 113
Fildes, 66
Firth, 65
Fisher, 89
Fletcher, 68, 136
Forsyth, 66-68
Foster, 78, 83, 148
Foulkes, 45
Foyster, 52, 69
Fraser, 62
Frier, 125
Frith, 131
Frodsham, 46
Fullalove, 45

Gadd, 113
Gallemore, 41, 56
Garner, 95, 99, 105, 114, 132, 135, 137, 139
Geisser, 131
Geissler, 46
Gibson, 58
Gladwin, 47
Golding, 132
Goodfellow, 88
Goodier, 93, 139-40
Gore, 47

Gough, 52, 117, 137
Gow, 54
Grantham, 31
Grasby, 47, 64
Gratrix, 118, 120, 122-24, 128, 132, 137-38, 140, 143
Green, 42
Greenall, 143
Greenhough, 46
Gresty, 118, 122-23, 128, 135, 143
Grimshaw, 89
Grundy, 82, 146

Hall, 44-45, 62, 131
Hallott, 88
Hamer, 59
Hamilton, 53, 63, 69
Hammond, 41, 147
Hamnett, 97, 102
Hampson, 37, 74, 88, 97, 114-15, 124, 126, 128, 133, 135, 143
Hancock, 80, 84, 101, 141, 143
Handley, 58
Hanmer, 54, 70
Hanson, 148
Hardwick, 145
Harrison, 39, 45, 77, 122, 126
Harrop, 32, 121, 124, 135, 138
Hartley, 114
Haslam, 32, 72, 78, 134
Hatfield, 147
Hawkins, 103
Haworth, 97, 101
Hayman, 102, 109, 143
Heald, 73, 78
Heap, 37
Heaps, 56, 132
Herriott, 83, 146
Hesketh, 21, 87, 89, 118, 122
Heslop, 45
Heward, 73, 77-78, 82, 136, 138
Hewitt, 36, 40, 52, 55, 136
Heyward, 74
Heywood, 32, 63, 104, 108, 111, 127, 132, 141
Hickin, 68

Hickman, 128, 132
Higgin, 103
Higgins, 73
Higson, 95, 99, 117, 137-38, 143
Hillkirk, 108, 136
Hime, 67
Hinde, 43
Hockenhull, 102
Hodgson, 26, 126, 131
Hogg, 111
Holland, 123
Hooton, 127
Hope, 34, 45
Horner, 69
Horrocks, 56
Horsfall, 85, 89
Houghton, 71
Howard, 61, 97
Howarth, 102, 121-22, 125-26, 130-31, 139, 147
Howes, 70
Howitt, 52, 131
Hoyle, 26, 87, 146
Hull, 113
Hulme, 32, 74, 140
Hunt, 56, 117
Hunter, 37, 97
Hurlbutt, 43, 53, 61, 118, 123
Hurst, 68

Ingram, 55, 67
Irlam, 31, 72, 74
Irwin, 64

Jackson, 53-54, 70-71, 81, 90
Johnson, 21, 26, 49, 59, 102, 108
Jolly, 87, 148
Jones, 65, 68-69, 104, 111
Joule, 66
Joynson, 22, 26, 40, 55-56, 145
Just, 147

Kay, 53, 146
Keal, 62, 70, 103, 113
Keith, 42
Kelly, 42, 104, 108

Kelsall, 37, 54, 74, 78, 95, 97, 102, 105, 114, 127, 128, 134, 138, 141
Kendall, 90, 111
Kennedy, 125, 147
Kenworthy, 68
Kerry, 68
Kilburn, 70
King, 46, 53, 128
Kinsey, 41, 56
Kirtley, 47, 89
Knight, 75, 142
Knowles, 62, 131
Kretchy, 66

Lamb, 21, 56-57, 67, 131
Lane, 101, 145
Larmuth, 70
Later, 49, 66, 68
Lee, 44, 63, 87, 134, 138
Leebridge, 74, 78, 146
Leech, 132
Leeds, 36, 56
Lees, 148
Legh, 20, 74-75, 95, 115, 118, 121, 124, 127, 136, 138, 141, 147
Leigh, 118, 123-24, 126-27, 131, 140
Lewis, 43
Lightbourne, 44
Lightfoot, 37
Lilly, 71
Litherland, 138
Little, 109, 144
Lloyd, 108
Lomas, 45, 67
Losh, 61, 85, 89
Luke, 66, 69
Lynde, 91
Lyon, 125, 148
Lyth, 122

Magson, 67
Maguire, 41
Markland, 45
Marple, 124, 128
Marsden, 42
Marsh, 46

Marsland, 19, 37, 39-40, 51, 55, 74, 78, 95, 97, 102, 108, 117-18, 122-23, 126, 128, 132, 136, 139, 142
Mason, 5, 61
Massey, 20, 35, 43, 59, 115, 117, 132
McClure, 46
McConnell, 130
McDougall, 70
McKenna, 42
Meadowcroft, 127
Medcalf, 126, 131
Mee, 137
Midwinter, 66
Midwood, 46, 54, 70, 145
Miller, 43, 66, 108
Milne, 83, 88, 130, 147
Mitchell, 62
Moore, 9, 40, 46, 52, 72, 74-75, 78, 80, 82, 97, 99, 105, 121, 126, 139, 146-48
Morgan, 88, 122, 131, 137, 141
Morley, 26, 52, 105
Morris, 32, 40, 44, 67, 137
Morrison, 46, 64
Mort, 115, 148
Moss, 93, 95, 143
Mothersill, 111
Moxon, 122, 126
Muir, 108
Murray, 88

Neill, 43, 51
Nelson, 141
Newton, 120, 148
Nicholson, 59
Nickson, 58
Nield, 78, 82
Noble, 59, 89
Nodal, 49
Norris, 111, 115 147

Occleston, 45
Ogden, 87, 146
Oldfield, 32, 36-37, 46, 123
Ollier, 39, 54, 71, 73, 105
Ollivant, 51, 66

Owen, 107, 143

Parker, 64, 109
Parkinson, 91
Parnell, 118, 126
Parr, 88
Parrish, 90
Peacock, 69
Pearn, 59
Pears, 75, 84
Pearson, 31, 65, 93, 125-26, 140, 143
Peel, 121, 125, 148
Pendlebury, 44, 68
Petremont, 42
Pettigrew, 91
Piggott, 45, 70
Pilling, 54, 145
Pixton, 109
Platt, 91
Pollard, 65
Pollitt, 62
Potter, 128, 131-32
Potts, 88, 126, 132
Price, 68
Prince, 103

Quinn, 91

Rae, 58
Radford, 103
Rampling, 147
Ratcliffe, 85
Ray, 26
Renshaw, 39, 47, 51, 54, 66, 71, 97, 102, 118, 120, 123, 138, 141, 143
Rhodes, 45, 55, 108
Richardson, 32, 36, 52, 57, 63-64, 78, 83, 87, 134
Ridyard, 43, 84, 88, 141
Roberts, 61, 90-91, 140
Robinson, 46, 55, 57
Robson, 88
Roby, 63
Roebuck, 39-40, 53-54, 70, 145, 146
Rogers, 63
Rooke, 58

Roylance, 118, 123, 141, 148
Royle, 31-32, 35, 37, 39, 49, 54, 74, 78, 80, 103, 118, 123, 143
Russell, 55, 59, 147
Ryder, 56
Rylance, 59, 65, 90

Sadler, 37
Sampson, 62
Sandbach, 57, 70
Sanders, 65
Sanderson, 53
Sargeant, 47
Scelland, 37, 39
Schiele, 68
Schofield, 118, 122, 140
Schutz, 83, 148
Scott, 66, 68, 109, 113, 145
Sedgeley, 65
Sharples, 71
Shaw, 88
Shawcross, 111, 124, 138
Shingles, 45
Shockledge, 51
Shore, 146
Siddall, 35, 146
Simpson, 107, 114, 139
Singleton, 80, 82, 136
Skaife, 85, 89
Skelton, 46
Slade, 84
Slater, 111
Smith, 58-59, 62, 65, 84, 89-90, 127-28, 131, 133, 136, 138, 140, 143, 146, 148
Southwell, 82, 83
Sowerby, 26, 37
Stafford, 51
Stamford, 20, 37, 74-75, 80, 93, 95, 97, 107, 117, 121, 137-38, 142-43, 146
Standring, 71
Statham, 84
Stevenson, 52
Storey, 26, 103, 109
Stracey, 58
Street, 69, 131

Strettell, 122, 140
Sutherland, 40, 55, 81, 84, 123, 127, 136
Sutton, 105
Swire, 82-83, 88

Taylor, 65, 75, 93, 101, 132, 139, 147
Tebbutt, 125, 130, 147
Thistlethwaite, 91
Thomas, 42
Thompson, 102, 107-08
Thornber, 26, 52, 66, 69
Thornhill, 109
Thorold, 75, 140
Thorpe, 61, 89
Timperley, 133, 138
Titmas, 62
Towler, 91
Tracey, 70
Trad, 63
Trafford, 121, 125, 147
Turner, 45
Twigge, 56, 69
Twiss, 54
Tyrer, 36, 40, 123
Tyson, 69

Underwood, 89
Unsworth, 64

Vassilopulo, 67

Waddell, 62
Wadsworth, 61
Walkden, 78, 133, 135, 139
Walker, 47, 51, 62, 67, 88
Warburton, 43, 113, 115
Ward, 82, 87
Wardle, 37, 51, 102
Wardleworth, 46, 65
Warren, 37, 42, 56
Warrens, 91
Warriner, 44, 90
Watkin, 26, 53
Watson, 91, 105

Wellford, 89
Wheatley, 41
Whichello, 47, 64
White, 20-21, 73, 78, 87-88, 115, 117, 120, 124, 131, 135, 138, 140, 142, 148
Whitehead, 75, 81-82, 84, 87, 93, 97, 123, 135, 138-39, 147
Whitelegg, 21, 31, 36, 54, 80, 83, 101, 118, 122, 126, 139-40
Whitmore, 83
Whittenbury, 82-83
Whitteron, 143
Whittle, 55
Whitwell, 115, 123
Whitworth, 46
Wight, 49, 69
Wilding, 71
Wilkinson, 59
Williams, 68
Williamson, 37, 59, 66, 95, 97, 134, 143
Wilson, 6, 26, 41, 51, 55-56, 69, 104
Winstanley, 21, 44, 52, 62, 88, 90
Witty, 68, 108-09
Wonstall, 58
Wood, 130-31, 140, 142, 147
Woodall, 37, 43, 74, 78, 80, 99, 105, 123, 127-28, 131, 136, 138, 143
Woodhead, 124, 146
Woodiwiss, 20, 135, 138
Woollaston, 45
Woolmore, 70
Worthington, 26, 65, 68, 87, 121, 125, 130, 138, 147-48
Wovenden, 57
Wright, 20, 55, 70, 95, 126, 130, 133, 135

Yarwood, 85, 132
Yates, 42, 62, 69, 97
Ydlibi, 71

Zahn, 54, 70, 145
Zill, 111

161

House Name Index

(includes terraces but not whole streets)

Abbot's Court, 140
Ada Terrace, 56, 132
Albion Villa, 52, 68
Allington Cottages, 125, 130
Alma Terrace, 46, 56, 64
Amery Vale, 113
Antonio's Villas, 69
Apna Villa, 61
Aroma Terrace, 17, 43, 51
Ashfield, 31, 36, 40, 55, 145
Audley House, 90
Avenham, 67

Banana Villas, 88
Bancroft's Houses, 80, 84
Bank Cottage, 71
Bank View, 130
Bankfield House, 69
Barracks, 123
Beaufort House, 104, 113
Beech Cottage, 39, 44
Beech House, 65, 108, 124, 128, 132
Beech Terrace, 44
Beech Villa, 49, 67
Beechfield, 89, 101, 107, 111, 145
Beechwood, 84, 89
Belmont, 66
Belmore, 111
Beswick Place, 85, 89
Birch Cottage, 103
Birch Lea, 70
Birch Villa, 68
Birchfield, 126
Boundary House, 124, 128
Bowdon View, 103
Brackenhoe, 63
Briarleigh, 61
Bridgewater Cottage, 41, 56
Brighton Place, 52
Broadoaks, 54, 70, 145
Brogden Grove, 113
Brogden Terrace, 113

Brook House, 55
Brookfield, 62, 108, 113
Brookfield House, 51, 68
Brooklands Cottage, 111
Brooklands House, 42, 104, 108
Brooklands Terrace, 111
Brooklands Villa, 111
Brooklyn Villa, 49
Brookside, 107
Broomfield, 67
Broomville, 67
Brunswick Villa, 41, 56

Cabbage Row, 36, 40, 56
Carlton Terrace, 113
Carlton Villas, 113
Cavendish Villa, 70
Clairville, 70
Claremont, 61, 63, 91, 113
Clarendon House, 63
Claydon House, 85, 89

Derby House, 52, 68
Dunham View, 103

Ebenezer House, 51, 66
East View, 113
Edwin Terrace, 56, 132
Ellan Brook, 90, 111
Ellesmere House, 65
Elm Terrace, 53
Elms, The, 67
Elsinore, 62
Enville Terrace, 45, 46, 59
Exeter House, 85, 89
'Eyebrow Cottage', 72, 78, 82, 87, 134, 145

Fernacre, 111
Fernbank, 127
Fern Lea, 67, 88
Ferrol Lodge, 61, 63

162

Glan-navan, 61
Glendale House, 63
Gorse Cottage, 56-57
Gosport Villa, 90
Green Bank, 69, 71
Greystoke, 90
Grove, The, 41, 56
Grove House, 87

Haddon Lodge, 70
Handley Terrace, 58
Harboro Villa, 107
Harper Hill, 56, 69
Harwood House, 88
Haworth House, 70
Hawthorn Cottage, 42, 56
Hazelmere Hotel, 59
Heathfield House, 51, 66
Heathville, 62
Hereford House, 59
Hermopolis, 67
Heywood Bank, 57
Hill End View, 114
Hiltly, 107, 132
Holly Bank, 52, 69, 105
Holly Cottage, 51
Holly Grove, 43, 61
Holly House, 85, 89
Holly Lodge, 63
Holly Villa, 43, 59
Hope Cottage, 102, 107-08
Hope Bank, 65
Hope Villa, 127
Horton Royde, 111
Howarth's Houses, 122
Huntley House, 62

Inglewood, 67
Inkerman Cottages, 44-45
Irlam View, 90
Ivy Cottage, 51, 54, 75, 84, 89

Johnson's Villa, 49

Kent Villa, 62

Landsdowne Terrace, 40
Laurel Bank, 47, 67
Laurel Cottage, 43, 59
Laurels, The, 58
Leamington Villas, 53, 70
Lee House, 61
Leigh Lodge, 67
Lily Bank, 59
Lime Place, 44-45, 59
Lime Villa, 49, 68
Lyme Grove, 103, 109
Lynwood Villas, 91

Marchfield Terrace, 49, 66
Marsholgate House, 46
Marsland Houses, 122
Massey Place, 125
Mayfield, 54, 67, 70, 126-27, 131
Meadow View, 127
Mersey Court, 74
Mersey Lea, 111
Midmoor Cottage, 59
Milton Cottage, 42, 56
Minerva House, 104, 109
Miry Gate House, 74, 78, 83, 145
Mitford House, 113
Model Cottages, 64
Moor Cottage, 97
Moorfield Cottage, 104, 108
Moorfield Place, 128
Moorlands, 90
Moorside, 58
Moss Bank, 70
Moss Cottage, 49, 68, 104
Moss Grove House, 51, 66
Mount Pleasant, 82, 87

New Chester, 39
North Bank, 62
North View, 90
Northern View, 51, 66
Northwood Cottage, 49, 68
Northwood House, 69
Northwood Lodge, 68
Norton Villa, 67
Oak Bank, 47, 127

Oak Cottage, 56
Oak House, 41, 56, 90
Oak Place, 36
Oak Terrace, 45
Oak Villa, 61, 68
Oaklands, 109
Oaklands House, 26, 56
Oaks, The, 126, 131
Old Hall Court, 117
Old Manor House, 72, 78, 82, 87, 145
Olive Grove, 44
Olive Mount, 62
Overdale, 66

Park Cottage, 51
Park House, 61
Park View, 103
Peace Terrace, 131
Pengwyn House, 130
Percival Terrace, 49, 68
Poole Croft, 122, 126
Poplar House, 42
Poplars, The, 56-57
Priory, The - see Sale Priory
Priory Bank, 82, 88
Priory Cottage, 83, 88
Priory Cottages, 84, 89
Priory Gate House, 74, 83, 87, 146
Priory Mount, 88-89
Priory Villa, 88
Prospect House, 59, 104

Raglan House, 102, 105, 107, 111
Renshaw Cottages, 54
Renshaw Fields, 43, 61
Renshaw Terrace, 43
Rio Cottage, 68
Riversdale, 90
Rock Villa, 59
Rose Bank, 64
Rose Lea, 68
Rose Villa, 49, 103
Roseville Cottage, 39, 54, 71
Rosslyn, 62
Roundland Cottage, 128
Roundland House, 104, 128

Roundland Terrace, 123, 132
Roundthorn, 61
Ryburn Villas, 88-89

Sale Bank, 39, 53, 70, 146
Sale Bank Cottage, 54, 71
Sale Bridge House, 64
Sale Cottage, 117, 121, 125, 130, 146
Sale Cottages, 36
Sale Green Cottages, 117, 121, 125
Sale Green House, 83
Sale Grove, 103
Sale Heys Cottage, 97, 101, 107, 147
Sale Lodge, 121, 125, 130-31, 147
Sale New Hall, 21, 74, 84, 117, 120, 122-23, 126, 130-31, 140
Sale Old Hall, 20, 78, 82, 115, 121, 123, 125, 126, 130, 138, 147
Sale Priory, 21, 73, 83, 87, 148
Sale Terrace, 39, 102
Salisbury House, 65
Sandal House, 113
Selbourne Lodge, 68
Sherrington House, 137
Shrewsbury House, 67
South Bank, 90
South View, 49
South Villas, 49, 68
Southfield House, 61, 63
Southfields, 102
Springfield House, 42, 56
Stamford Terrace, 45-46, 59
Stanley Bank, 42
Stanley House, 108
Stanley Place, 43
St. Margaret's View, 114
Stoneleigh, 89
Stowey, 90
Strawberry Bank, 44
Summer Villa, 49
Summerlea, 62
Summerville, 87
Sunny Bank, 66
Sunnyside, 70
Swiss Villas, 68
Sylvan Villa, 64

164

Syrian Villa, 64

Tatham House, 108
Temple, The, 17, 34, 37, 43, 46
Temple Villa, 47
Temple Terrace, 47
Thorn Grove House, 65
Thorncliffe, 62
Thornfield, 89-90
Thornhill, 67
Thorn Lea, 67

Vanner House, 59
Ventnor Villa, 61
Vermont, 62
Vernon Lodge, 51, 103
Victoria Cottage, 44, 59, 62, 132
Victoria Place, 52

Wallbank Terrace, 125, 126, 130, 132

Warburton House, 43
Wardle House, 52, 66, 143
Waterside Cottages, 21, 122
West Bank, 53
Windsor Cottage, 53, 105
Winterholme, 90
Woodbourne, 111
Woodheys, 101, 107, 148
Woodland Cottages, 84
Woodlands, 67
Woodley Bank, 89
Woodrose Cottages, 132
Woodville, 42, 104

Yew Tree Cottage, 84, 89, 118, 123, 128, 132, 135
Yew Villas, 57, 68, 70
York Terrace, 58

Zizinia's Villas, 69